Battlefield Ramadi: A Story of Modern Infantry

By Jeremy A. Stokely

ISBN: 979-8-9888970-2-6 (Paperback)
ISBN: 979-8-9888970-3-3 (eReader)

Library of Congress Control Number: 2025901826

First printing edition March 2025

Sand & Grit Publishing Company
Hutchinson, KS 67502

IG: @shoot_move_and_medicate
jeremystokely@gmail.com

Table of Contents

For infantrymen past and present.

Author's Foreword

If you're expecting a perfectly polished, detail-heavy narrative filled with non-mission-related anecdotes, this book isn't for you. But if you're searching for an unfiltered, first-hand account of the sheer chaos and brutality that young infantrymen endure daily during deployment, then buckle up—this is your book.

In 2020, for the first time in over 15 years, I opened the journal I had kept throughout my time in Iraq from 2004 to 2005. Reading it was a mix of shock and nostalgia. I laughed out loud at the absurdity and nonchalance with which I described events that, looking back, seem surreal. The journal, admittedly, isn't comprehensive; I wish I had recorded more. Some stories here may seem exaggerated or impossible, but I promise you, every account is true. While some missions have been combined for a smoother narrative, everything depicted happened as described. Dialogue is reconstructed from my memory and that of my platoon, staying true to the spirit of what was said, even if the exact words might have shifted with time.

Some memories are crystal clear for one or two of us, while others have been forgotten by many—a testament to the varied ways we cope. But it's essential that people understand the reality for young soldiers in combat roles overseas.

A common misconception is that all military personnel engage in frontline combat. In reality, only a small percentage of the massive U.S. Armed Forces make up combat arms. Support units play an indispensable role in the war effort, facing danger now and then, but their experiences differ from those of infantrymen who spend most of their time "outside the wire."

Unlike books about famous missions, elite units, or Medal of Honor recipients, this story is about the everyday grunt—the "Joe" in the trenches. "Joe" is a term we used for lower enlisted soldiers, often with an edge of endearment and sarcasm. If you asked me who is most likely to see action, my answer would always be the same: an 11B, an infantryman. Not a member of some elite unit—though many aspire to that—but regular, run-of-the-mill infantry.

I was an average soldier, far from the type to make it into a ranger battalion or special forces. I probably couldn't have passed the 5-mile run for airborne school, but I earned my Combat Infantry Badge many times over, no exaggeration. Our platoon statistics at the end of deployment spoke volumes: over 100 combat missions, more than 70 enemy engagements, not including countless IED (improvised explosive device - i.e. roadside bomb) encounters. I'm sure similar experiences could be shared by every infantry platoon in Ramadi, whether Army or Marines.

This isn't a book about leadership or military strategy—I was a 19-year-old private, a private first class in name only. I didn't know the grand mission or even the company's goals half the time. I was just a grunt, and that's the perspective this book is written from: the view of a young soldier doing his job, no more, no less.

To piece this together, I reached out to as many of my platoon members as possible. Some were eager to contribute, some remained silent but clearly saw my messages on social media when I tried contacting them, and a few wanted no part of it, or to not even have their name mentioned, which I respected. Without those who shared their memories, this book wouldn't exist. Some stories were recalled differently by those involved, but I did my best to capture each moment as faithfully as possible, even when memories varied. While our story isn't vastly different from that of any other infantry platoon in Iraq in 2004, it is ours, and I believe it deserves to be told.

This story primarily follows my squad, but the rest of the platoon is frequently mentioned because, in the military, your platoon is your family—the ones you share every mission with. There were countless stories that couldn't be included in this book, and with 35 to 40 men in a platoon, naming everyone individually would have been impossible. As much as I wanted to, it would have become overwhelming and confusing. However, I do mention several soldiers outside my squad who were invaluable in helping me piece this book together. Their memories, often sharper than my own, naturally include moments involving themselves.

I am self-publishing and self-editing this book, fully aware that editing your own work is not ideal. However, I lack three critical resources: time, money, and patience. I work full-time, attend school full-time in a psychiatric mental health nurse practitioner program, run a small screen printing business, and serve in the Kansas Air National Guard. This schedule leaves me with precious little time. While I manage financially, I don't have the thousands of dollars required to hire even the most affordable, reputable editor to review my manuscript. Some might say I should have found a way to make it work, but to them, I say: write your own book—this one is mine.

Patience, or the lack thereof, is perhaps my biggest hurdle. I started this book three years ago, but the first draft sat untouched for two years before I finally decided to complete it. I'm not willing to wait any longer to share these stories. This book was never intended to be a polished masterpiece; it was a way for me to process and confront the emotional weight of my first deployment—a deeply therapeutic endeavor. An editor would likely advise me to focus more on character development to give readers a better understanding of the people in the story. But for me, it's not about any one individual; it's about the shared experiences of all young soldiers, Marines, and even sailors and airmen who face combat on a nearly daily basis. These stories, all true, don't belong solely to my platoon. Every infantry platoon in Ramadi from 2004 to 2005, whether Army or Marine, dealt with the same chaos we did. It was an extraordinary time.

I hope that despite the imperfections and rawness, readers will find something meaningful in this book, no matter how professional or polished it appears.

Intro

What's it like to be infantry? I'll tell you, but it's not sexy. We weren't Rangers or Navy SEALs. We didn't wear green berets or belong to any elite, secretive unit. We weren't the vaunted tip of the spear that so many other units claimed to be. Hell, we weren't even airborne. We were light infantry, cobbling together a sort of mounted hybrid force, riding in semi-armored Humvees—on days we weren't marching straight out the front gate and into hell.

We wore body armor stuffed with magazines and pouches bulging with grenades that seemed to itch for action. Carbines and squad automatic weapons were slung across our chests, instruments of war waiting to be played. Each shot a note in the chaotic symphony of combat. Every note performed with the pull of a trigger. The M240s and .50 caliber machine guns roared with beauty, anchoring that symphony with a low, relentless thrum. We were nightmares made real for our enemies.

Bravery was our uniform, worn like the latest fashion trend, too young to understand that courage often courts death. Blue cords on our shoulders bore the weight of all that was asked of us. We were ground-pounding, knuckle-dragging freedom fighters, answering Uncle Sam's call with unyielding resolve. Not the most skilled or educated soldiers the Army had to offer—but damned if we weren't the proudest. We fought until ordered to stop, and sometimes, even then, we didn't.

We were the queen of battle. We were eleven bravos. We were grunts. We were infantry. Maybe, just maybe, it was a little sexy after all.

Chapter 1

Dancing with fire

March 1st, 2005 - Just before sunset

I look down as fire and smoke dance across the floor, waltzing along with every stomp of my combat boots. Flames creep up the driver-side window, warping the glass, twisting it like wax in the heat. My humvee is burning to the ground, and I'm stuck inside. I throw my shoulder against the door with everything I've got, but it doesn't budge, mocking my efforts. My rifle, slung across my chest, catches on the radio mount, trapping me in this furnace. Each breath feels like inhaling razor blades as smoke fills my lungs, but it's the heat that really burns—a blazing wall pressing in from all sides, suffocating, relentless. Everything is melting, even the illusion of invincibility I'd wrapped myself in. In the chaos, something unfamiliar and ugly roots itself in my bones—panic.

Minutes Earlier

Third platoon is navigating the narrow streets of southeastern Ramadi, heading to exfil scouts from Ghost platoon holed up in a bombed-out building. It's getting close to sunset, and shadows are lengthening across every alley and wall, turning the entire city into a deathtrap. This place is vicious, and it's already claimed too many American lives. The mood in each humvee is tense;

everyone's got their eyes peeled, waiting for anything to twitch wrong.

Staff Sergeant Dubose, in the lead truck, slows to a stop and radios back to Lieutenant Chappell in the next vehicle.

"This is a bad idea, LT. We should go around."
But the LT is confident, almost too casual.

"Just speed through. It'll be fine."

Dubose grips the wheel tighter, eyes scanning the unpaved dirt path littered with trash, rocks, and an abandoned car that looks like it's been rotting there since the last war. This place is perfect for an ambush. Every instinct is screaming at me to turn back, to find another way.

But we press on. The lead humvee inches forward, headlights cutting through the gathering dark, tires kicking up clouds of dust. In front of us lies nothing but loose dirt—no hardball to keep us clear of IEDs—and piles of trash flank both sides of the road, practically begging for something nasty to be hiding inside. An Improvised Explosive Device (IED) is a homemade bomb, often hidden in roads, vehicles, or debris, designed to ambush and destroy. In Iraq, they were the deadliest threat, capable of shredding vehicles and killing instantly.My gut twists as we creep closer to that burnt-out car sitting near the end of the path, almost like it's waiting for us. I glance at Sergeant Brown.

"Hey, I'm gonna let them get almost to the end before I go, okay?" I say.
"Sounds good, Stoke," he replies, nodding, his eyes sharp.

As soon as the lead vehicles clear the dirt path, I slam the gas, the humvee lurching forward as I try to put as much distance as I can. The whole area feels wrong, and every inch closer feels like stepping onto a trap. My skin prickles, and there's this crawling sensation that something is about to go off. I press the pedal harder, asking God to keep us safe.

Three-quarters of the way down, the whole world explodes. The blast slams into the humvee with bone-breaking force. Fire and debris erupt around me, throwing the burnt-out car's roof high into the air as a massive shockwave rattles everything loose. Shrapnel punches through the doors, and I'm engulfed in a wall of flames, metal twisting and screaming as the whole vehicle buckles around me. Every bone in my body vibrates from the impact, and my ears are ringing so loud it drowns out the chaos outside. I'm dazed, head pounding, trying to make sense of what just happened.

"Fuck! Whoever's in the 998 is fucking dead!" Private First Class Schuh shouts from the gunner's turret two trucks back, his voice frantic.

Back to the Present

I slam my shoulder into the door again and again, desperate to escape, but it's jammed, refusing to move. Flames are licking up the sides, the heat radiating off the walls, mocking every failed attempt. I hit it a third time, and finally, it gives. I fall out, my vision blurring from smoke, my lungs seizing as I gasp for fresh air. I stumble onto the dirt, feeling the sting of scrapes, cuts, and bruises, but I'm alive, and for a moment, that's all that matters.

The gunner in the fourth vehicle has already radioed for a medic, but I don't need it. Not yet, anyway. I'm too dazed to process what's next, confusion clouding every thought, my vision still blurred and ringing in my ears louder than any command. I spin around, trying to find my footing, heart hammering as I realize I haven't checked on Sergeant Brown. Where the hell is Brown? My body moves on instinct, eyes scanning for threats while my mind struggles to catch up. The house directly in front of me has its gate open, and with my rifle at the ready, I push forward and clear the small courtyard.

The silence is unnatural, broken only by the crackling fire behind me and the muffled, frantic voices over the radio. The courtyard seems empty, and reality comes crashing back into me. Brown. Where's Brown? A cold fear grips me as I remember the explosion, replaying in flashes that make my hands tremble.

Unbeknownst to me, I egressed so quickly that Brown, in the immediate chaos, assumed I had been blown right out of the humvee—another KIA balled up on the side of the road. Time feels like it's stretched thin; what felt like minutes of panic was only seconds. Brown escapes the vehicle, dirt and debris still falling around him, and his boot kicks up a patch of loose dirt that exposes wires leading to an unexploded 155mm shell on his side of the humvee. My heart skips when I realize how close we came to being sandwiched between two massive explosions. Thank God it didn't blow. Brown doesn't waste time. He rounds the back of the humvee, scanning for me, expecting the worst. When he doesn't see me sprawled out in the dirt, hope flares up. His eyes dart around the scene, finally catching sight of me in the courtyard, coughing, rifle in hand, but alive. Relief washes over him, but only for a moment. He freezes, then turns abruptly back to the burning truck.

From Lieutenant Chappell's vehicle, Private First Class Mullins watches with a mix of shock and disbelief as Brown heads back toward the humvee.

"Leave the fucking rifle, dude!" Mullins yells, eyes wide.

"Mullins, what the fuck is Brown doing?!" the LT snaps, leaning out of the window, trying to piece together the chaos unraveling in front of him.

"He left his rifle in the truck! He's going back for it!"

Smoke curls around Brown as he disappears into the heat and debris, ignoring Mullins and the LT. Seconds feel like hours until he reappears, M4 clutched in one hand, his other arm shielding his face from the searing smoke. He's coughing, hacking up what seems like half his lungs, but he doesn't slow until he reaches the courtyard, where I'm still standing, chest heaving.

"Stoke, you okay?!" His voice is hoarse, strained.

"I'm good, Sergeant. Are you?!"

"Yeah, I'm good." He coughs again, and we take a moment to pat each other down, hands shaking as we check for injuries.

A superficial cut on my left hand and arm, the throbbing pain in my knee, elbow, and shoulder—not great, but not bad enough to stop me. We're both breathing, and that's more than enough.

Before we can process anything further, Sergeant Dubose emerges from his humvee, eyes scanning the wreckage with the urgency of someone who's seen this kind of hell too many times. He shouts orders, calling first Squad's Bravo team to set up on a rooftop a few houses down from my position.

"Moret, you're with me, let's go!" Dubose commands, his voice steady and commanding, cutting through the chaotic noise.

Moret follows, and together they round the corner and find us still catching our breath, adrenaline still spiking through our veins.

"You guys good? What the fuck happened?" Dubose barks as he steps into the courtyard, eyes darting between us and the burning humvee.

"We're good, Sergeant," I say, my voice steadying as reality settles over me like a heavy blanket. "Now what?"

"You sure? Need a medic to check you out?" Dubose's eyes narrow, searching for any sign we're more beat up than we're letting on.

"No, man. We're good," Brown replies, wiping sweat and soot from his brow.

Dubose glances back at the humvee, eyes narrowing as he takes in the wreckage.

"I thought that was the fucking LT's truck that blew."

The distant echo of gunfire suddenly reminds us the fight isn't over. Not yet, anyway.

The Smoke Clears...Almost

The world has gone eerily silent after the explosion, only the faint crackle of burning metal and the distant hum of engines breaking the stillness. Then, the front door of the house whose courtyard we are occupying creaks open, and a small boy steps out, his gaze wide but calm, carrying a piece of cloth. His mother watches from the doorway, her face a mix of fear and curiosity. As the boy reaches me, he begins to wipe the soot from my face, like I'm some lost traveler instead of a filth-covered soldier. His touch is gentle, like he's trying to erase the horrors I just walked out of and for a split second, all the tension in my body disappears, replaced by a strange calm. The moment is surreal, almost holy in its own way.

I'm speechless. For a moment, everything fades—the fire, the screams, the adrenaline pumping through my veins. But just as quickly, the moment shatters. A crack rings out, high and sharp. AK-47 fire.

I grab the boy by his shoulders, urging him back into his house, but he presses the cloth into my hand, as calm as if we were standing anywhere else but a war zone. I stuff it into my pocket, something to remember—a reminder of humanity in the middle of hell.

Bravo team from my squad is already in position, weapons aimed at every corner, every rooftop. The streets are a maze, and the insurgents know every turn and hiding spot. They have the advantage, and they know it, picking us off from angles we can't see, firing and then vanishing into the next block like ghosts.

Up on the rooftop, Sweeney lies flat, his SAW balanced on the ledge, eyes fixed on the alley ahead. The M249 Squad Automatic Weapon (SAW) is a light machine gun that provides rapid, sustained fire to suppress enemies and support infantry squads. He catches a flicker of movement—a man in a ski mask, peeking out from around the corner.

"Sergeant Hicks, get over here," Sweeney whispers, barely moving his eyes from the target.

"What do you got, Sweeney?" Hicks asks, crouching beside him.

"Intersection, a hundred meters out. Dude in a ski mask, but I can't tell if he's armed," Sweeney mutters, eyes narrowing.

"Isn't a guy in a mask free game?"

"Just keep a close eye on it," Hicks replies, tension building.

The insurgent reappears, this time with something long and dark in his hands—a weapon. Without waiting for a further command, Sweeney steadies his grip, adrenaline kicking in.

"He's about to shoot!" Sweeney hisses.

"Well, shoot him then!" Hicks barks.

Sweeney's SAW roars to life, tracer rounds lighting up the night as bullets shred through the alleyway. The masked man staggers from a hit, followed by another insurgent darting out, then dragging him behind cover. Sweeney keeps firing, the SAW jerking in his grip as he peppers the walls, each shot an attempt to put down anyone who dares show their face.

Down below, King's truck takes fire, bullets raking across the windshield and turret. King's gunner, Schuh, opens up with the M240, spraying rounds down the alley. The M240 is a belt-fed, 7.62mm medium machine gun used by U.S. forces for superior firepower, capable of sustained, accurate fire to suppress and engage enemy targets. The firefight intensifies, gunfire echoing off the walls as the insurgents disappear into the maze.

Pursuit Through the Streets

With the insurgents on the run, Sergeant Dubose motions to us, and we move in, ducking into alleys, guns at the ready, adrenaline pumping. I'm alongside Brown, Moret, and the rest, boots pounding the dirt as we sprint through the narrow lanes. Each corner could be hiding more insurgents, and we cover each other, moving fast and tight, our rifles up, scanning every doorway, every rooftop.

"Let's go! We can catch 'em!" I shout, barely able to hear my own voice over the chaos.

"Where are they?" someone calls.

"Anybody got eyes?" another voice shouts back.

As we press forward, the tension rises, the city closing in around us, each alley feeling like a trap waiting to spring. Another burst of gunfire erupts, and we hit the ground, pressing ourselves against walls, eyes scanning the rooftops. Moret, our SAW gunner, opens up, spraying rounds across a suspected hiding spot. We leapfrog forward, moving as a single unit, covering each other, pushing further into the maze.

After several blocks, Dubose finally signals for us to hold, his face set in frustration. The insurgents are gone, slipped back into the shadows like ghosts.

"What an incredible waste of energy," he mutters.

We're drenched in sweat, bruised and pissed, the adrenaline wearing off and leaving only exhaustion in its place.

Reflections in the Dark

The sun has set by the time we head back to base, and that hollow, bone-deep exhaustion settles in, but it's more than just fatigue. I slump into the back of one of our few up-armored humvees, knees pulled to my chest, feeling like I'm finally unmasking a fear I'd been pretending didn't exist.

For the last seven months, I hadn't felt fear—not once. Not after sitting through service after service for fallen brothers, not after watching guys in my own squad get shot up, and not even after packing up Doc Meyers' things to send home to his family. I'd told myself I was invincible, that the bad shit only happened to other people. Even when I got hurt, it never really shook me. I was still standing. Still breathing. Still here.

But tonight? Tonight was different.

For the first time, I knew—*really* knew—that I could die here. That at any moment, an IED, a sniper, a lucky RPG, or some shitbag with an AK hidden in a market stall could wipe me off the face of the earth. And it wouldn't be some heroic, last-stand, blaze-of-glory kind of death. It would be random. Instant. A flash of light, a burst of sound, and then nothing.

As we drive back, I can't shake the thought that an IED could go off at any moment, finishing the job that the last one started. My hands start to shake, and I pull my knees tighter to my chest, curling up like a kid hiding from monsters. Only this time, the monsters are real, and they're everywhere. I talk to God the whole way back, silently begging Him not to let another IED blow us up tonight.

Why are we even here? I signed up to rid the world of men like these, to put bullets into the evil hiding in dark places. But all I see are families caught in the crossfire, houses we've broken into searching for insurgents that never seem to be there. I'm just...tired. So damn tired.

As we pull into Camp Corregidor without further contact, I finally exhale, my hands still shaking. I uncurl myself from the seat and gather my thoughts, but I don't know how I'm going to keep doing this. Sergeant Dubose looks at me with that understanding, unsaid look. He tells me to take it easy for the night, and Sergeant First Class Cromer gives me permission to find the shower key. It's a small, rare luxury out here, but tonight, it feels like a lifeline.

I'm grateful as I walk back to my rack, still smelling of smoke and dirt. And even though my body's wired from the day's events, I know I won't sleep tonight. So instead, I sit down, pick up a pen, and start writing down everything that happened—the explosions, the firefight, the kid with the cloth—before the memories fade.

This wasn't the beginning of my deployment. It was closer to the end. And yet, in a way, this night *was* a beginning—the moment where I stopped believing I was untouchable. The moment I realized I wasn't just playing a deadly game. I could die in it.

Many missions have passed, and more will come. I'll keep kicking in doors, keep laughing with the guys, keep bitching about the heat, and keep dreaming about ice-cold Dr Pepper and home. But something changed in me after tonight. I stopped thinking of myself as invincible.

Because I wasn't.

None of us were.

Chapter 2

First Contact

September 15th, 2004

It's been just under two weeks since we touched down at Al-Taqaddum Air Base, TQ. For now, we're living in Habbaniyah, a dusty town sandwiched between Ramadi to the west and Fallujah to the east. Both cities are known for insurgent activity, but Ramadi, our target tonight, has a reputation as the most hostile place in Iraq. So far, our missions out of Habbaniyah have been small operations in surrounding villages – just enough to get our feet wet, but nothing too serious. Not until tonight.

We're staged at Camp Ramadi, preparing to roll into the heart of the city, and the tension is thick. The air smells like burning trash and diesel, with a faint hint of the sweat that's soaking through every uniform. The sand clings to everything, gritty between our teeth and coating our skin. Across from us, the armored personnel carrier – APC for short – looms like a steel beast, its back hatch open wide. It's waiting to swallow us up and haul us straight into the lion's den.

My squad leader, Staff Sergeant Dubose, keeps a watchful eye on his two team leaders, Sergeant Arcebuche, known as Archie, and Sergeant Hicks, as they run through final pre-combat checks. Dubose is a country boy, a hunter from back home who looks almost at ease in the chaos. Archie is Filipino, our only combat vet, and Hicks, one of the few black guys in our platoon, who always talks about using his "pimp hand" which cracks me up, is my team leader. The rest of us are a mixed bunch, a walking poster for Army diversity: there's Private First Class YellowHammer, a towering Native American; Private First Class Moret, my best friend and a mix of black and Filipino; Private First Class Cassell, who smokes like a chimney, Private First Class Patterson, a redheaded kid from Wisconsin who is a fellow guitar player; Private First Class Zangaro, who could easily pass for Italian but I never ask his ethnicity. We eventually gain Private First Class Sweeney, a bit of a nerd but a good guy, and Sergeant Brown, another dark-skinned guy who cracks me up because his name is Marc but would joke that he wished his parents would have named him DeShawn or something with more blackness, and then there's me, a Kansas boy who joined up at eighteen for adventure and to serve my country. Our little group of misfits is patched together from last-minute platoon swaps before deploying, making us the bastard child of Dog Company, 1st Battalion, 503rd Infantry. We happen to love our new step parents.

Tonight, we're crammed into a steel box on tracks, and the reality of where we're headed is sinking in fast. "Load up, men," Dubose orders, his voice even but firm.
We pile into the APC, and as the rear hatch closes, it feels like we're being sealed in. The cab is cramped, pitch dark, and stifling, the air thick with the metallic smell of gear and sweat. The APC rumbles beneath us, a twelve-ton beast with a .50 caliber machine gun mounted on top, a combat taxi built to take small arms fire and possible small IEDs and RPGs, but little else. Around us, the steel shell feels claustrophobic, pressing in as if daring us to breathe. The roof is open, which gives us the option to stand and fire if it comes to that, but it also means we're exposed if anything heavy comes our way.

15

Dubose sits across from me, eyes scanning us as if he's mentally preparing himself for anything. Across from me, YellowHammer is barely fitting in his seat, his massive frame practically overflowing into the space next to him. Patterson is beside me, pale but grinning, trying to shake off the nervous energy.

We feel the APC start to roll forward, and the motion sickness kicks in almost immediately. It's not the thought of combat making me nauseous – it's the heat and the confined space. Back in South Korea, we were light infantry, used to walking everywhere with our LPCs, or leather personnel carriers (that's combat boots for the uninitiated). Here, half our missions are still on foot alone but all the others,like tonight, it's the APC and humvees that get us around, and my stomach hates it. We lurch along, the treads of the APC grinding against the dirt road, and it's all I can do to keep from puking. I would not last in a mechanized infantry unit. Give me combat boots and direction and I will march until I am told to quit. Put me in a steel box and I hate my life.

The convoy winds its way through the outskirts of Camp Ramadi, and I can feel the tension building with every mile. Ramadi – they call it the Wild West of Iraq, a place where the insurgents run the show. It sits smack in the heart of the Sunni Triangle, and I know it's home to a special breed of fighters. I think back to the PowerPoint presentation we got on Iraqi culture, but honestly, the details are fuzzy. Sunni, Shiite – all I know is that they're not the enemy; it's the radicals, the Mujahideen, the Muj. And in Ramadi, they're waiting.

The closer we get, the more I feel that strange calm that settles in before chaos. The pre-mission jitters are gone, replaced by a laser focus. Patterson shifts beside me, and in the low light, I can see him glancing around, taking in every face. It's quiet – the calm before the storm.

Finally, the convoy turns onto Route Michigan, a road infamous for ambushes, the main artery slicing through Ramadi. It's hard to describe, but there's an energy to the city that feels dark and menacing, like it's watching us. Suddenly, flares shoot into the sky ahead, lighting up the night. The Muj knows we're coming. They're sending out the signal, calling in their own, and my pulse kicks up a notch.

Dubose's voice cuts through the tense silence, "Keep low and stay in the cab."

Next to me, YellowHammer shifts, his fingers twitching near his SAWs trigger.

"Let me get up there, sarn't," he mutters, itching to stand and take aim over the hatch.

"Stay the fuck where you are, Yellow," Dubose growls, yanking him back down before he can expose himself.

As we press deeper into the city, the APC grinds to an abrupt halt. Dubose looks down the lot of us and shouts, "Contact front!" but before the words even register, tracer rounds slice through the air just above our heads, their green light illuminating the cab in eerie, pulsing flashes.

Patterson's voice is excited but nervous, "Are we actually getting shot at?"

Dubose, not missing a beat, shouts back, "Yes, Patterson, we're being *fucking shot at!*"

The cab is alive with sound – bullets hammering the sides of the APC, each impact a metallic "ping." Sparks fly as rounds ricochet off the top hatch, and Combat Betty,

17

our loyal water cooler, takes a hit spraying us as if in protest. Water trickles down like rain inside the cramped cab and Combat Betty is the first in the squad to earn a purple heart. Well, that's not true actually, Archie was injured by a landmine in his first deployment prior to joining the 503rd. Next to me, Patterson's face lights up with awe as he stares at the tracer rounds – green, not red, like nothing we've seen before. It's like we're watching fireworks, except we're the target. Bullets rake the side of our APC, and even in the thick of it, I can't help but think about the guys in the cargo humvee directly behind us – they're practically unprotected.

The M998 cargo humvee was supposed to be reinforced with steel plates, but that hasn't happened yet. Right now, it's little more than wooden slats in the truck bed, with Kevlar blankets draped over the sides like a half-hearted attempt at armor. Enemy fire pounds against the makeshift protection, and I catch a glimpse of a water case near the front exploding in a spray of plastic and water. PFC Avery doesn't even realize it yet, but a bullet has punched clean through his sleeve.

"Stay tight and get the fuck down!" Sergeant Rogers shouts at Avery, Johnson, and Lineweber, his voice a lifeline in the chaos as they cling to whatever cover they can find.

The unmistakable roar of a .50 cal suddenly jolts me back to the present – but it's not coming from our APC. I realize it's PFC Cheney, two humvees back, laying down suppressive fire on the enemy. But our own gunner is silent? Is our gunner hit? No – he's squatting down, face flushed with fear, looking terrified. It's a stark contrast to the expressions on the rest of us, and I feel a flash of frustration. I briefly think to myself "what a lack of courage," but then again, I am well protected at the moment. We do, however, need that .50 to return fire. But the dude is not infantry; he's a middle-aged transportation specialist from the National Guard. He probably has a wife and kids back home – arguably more to lose. I've got nothing against Guard guys; they can stand toe-to-toe with any active-duty soldier most days but that's not the point. Right now, we need him firing, not cowering.

Cheney's still going strong with his .50 cal, blasting away as our APC lurches into a sharp left turn. Behind us, PFC Sikonia, at the wheel of the 998, doesn't see the turn until it's too late. The cargo humvee takes fire just as heavily as we are, only they have next to no armor to protect them. Sikonia hunches down as far as he can in the driver's seat, ducking low to avoid any rounds that might punch through the unarmored roof. Through his night vision goggles, he watches in stunned silence as hundreds of bullets chew into the APC ahead, then shift to hammer the side of his own 998.

"Oh, fuck! Oh, fuck! Oh, fuck!" Sikonia chants under his breath, his grip white-knuckled on the wheel.

With nerves shot and adrenaline spiking, Sikonia misjudges the turn and can't slow down in time. He yanks the wheel, sending the humvee up onto two wheels in a scene straight out of a Hollywood chase. For a few breathless seconds, the 998 teeters dangerously on its side before slamming back down, rocking the soldiers inside like rag dolls.

Then, Cheney's .50 cal goes silent, and for a moment, everything is still. The insurgents are likely dead before they hit the ground, torn apart by rounds of 7.62

and .50 cal. As I sit there, catching my breath, I realize the intense dislike I had for riding in an APC is starting to fade. This combat taxi just took heavy automatic weapons fire like a champ.

Captain Chu, our company commander, orders another platoon to search the building we took fire from, but they're already tied up. So he turns to us. Our squad of dismounts is now first in line for an impromptu building clearing. I guess our original objective can wait.

As the APC thunders toward the complex, Dubose tells the driver to angle the hatch toward one of the building's walls, avoiding any chance of a machine gunner opening up straight into the cab. As the hatch lowers, thoughts of storming the beach at Normandy flash through my mind, but Dubose has us covered with a safer direction for dismount.

Dubose's voice snaps me back to reality, "Dismount!"

We spill out of the APC, boots slamming onto the ground, weapons drawn, heads swiveling to scan every inch of the street. The air is thick with smoke, and the glow of burning cars flickers like ghostly lanterns down the block. The insurgents have disappeared, but we're on high alert. A car sits engulfed in flames, the metal warped and hissing as we pass. Somewhere nearby, the sound of gunfire crackles, not so distant but certainly urgent.

Dubose calls out, directing us toward a building where we think the enemy fire came from. When third squad catches up with first we move together towards the objective and it's clear that the bottom level is storefront property. We pass a barbershop that we will return to shortly with intel of weapons hidden there. Lt. Chappell orders us in once we reach the front entrance.

"Get in the building!" the LT shouts.

My entire squad, caught up in the moment, stacks on the front entrance. One lucky shot with an RPG, rocket-propelled grenade or a talented machine gunner, could have put bullet holes through each of us in seconds.

Lt. Chappell runs along beside us trying to psych us up for our first real door-kicking extravaganza. He later jokes about how silly it was but at the time it was working. Sergeant Dubose joins the party.

"Alright, boys! This is what we are getting paid for! Let's Go!"

The door is breached, and Sergeant Archie is the first one through, sweeping his sector to the left, his movements precise and deliberate. The rest of Alpha and Bravo teams follow close behind, moving with an efficiency that feels more instinctual than practiced. My thumb hovers just below my rifle's selector switch, itching to flip it to "fire" at the slightest sign of movement. We're tailed by Dubose, Lieutenant Chappell, and our interpreter, and every footfall feels loud against the silent, empty walls.

"Clear!" Archie calls, his voice echoing through the dark, lifeless room.

He says it out of habit, a reassurance to all of us. We know it's empty, but this is our first real combat mission with the possibility of enemy contact – no one's about to get lazy.

"Dubose, get your squad upstairs and start clearing rooms!" Lt. Chappell barks, motioning us forward.

We make our way toward a narrow side stairwell that feels almost claustrophobic. Clearing a stairwell takes patience and focus, usually just a few soldiers at a time. But as we climb to the top of the first floor, things get complicated. The stairwell splits, branching up and down, both forward and back. It's a tangled mess, and we adjust on the fly – one squad stays to secure the second floor while the rest of us push up toward the third.

The climb feels endless, and with each step, the tension builds. My mind is racing, anticipating threats that never materialize. As we reach the third-floor foyer, we're greeted by wary residents peeking out from behind cracked doors, eyes wide and faces pale. They're terrified, and I don't blame them; a squad of heavily armed American soldiers just stormed into their lives, and we don't look like we're here for a friendly chat. The space isn't more storefronts like we expected – it's an apartment complex.

We don't have to force any doors open. Most are already ajar, the residents too afraid to lock themselves in. We move room by room, checking each one quickly, keeping our presence known but restrained. With the second and third floors now secured, and no signs of the enemy, Dubose signals us to move up. We're heading to the rooftop, the likely vantage point from where they fired on us.

The last stairwell feels different – every creak and echo amplified by the silence around us. My pulse quickens as we near the rooftop access, knowing the enemy could be just beyond the final door.

"It's way too quiet," Archie whispers, barely loud enough for me to hear as he inches closer to the last door separating us from the rooftop.

"I know what you mean," Cassell whispers back, his voice tense. "We should have made contact by now."

The silence is thick, unsettling, as if the building itself is holding its breath. We wait, ready, not knowing what's waiting for us beyond that final door.

Archi, leading the charge, gives a nod to YellowHammer. "Get up here.. Make that door open," he whispers, and YellowHammer steps forward, his broad frame filling the narrow stairwell.

"Roger, sarn't," he grunts, gripping the handle. He's ready to swing it open, and we're ready to pour in.

With a quick shove, YellowHammer flings the door wide, and we rush out onto the rooftop, rifles at the ready, each of us covering a different sector. But instead of a firefight, we're greeted by... nothing. The place is deserted. The rooftop, bare and exposed, stretches out before us, littered with chunks of broken concrete, bullet holes pockmarking the low walls, and scattered rubble. Whoever was here has melted into the night, leaving behind only the remnants of a firefight.

"Where the fuck is everybody?" Dubose mutters, scanning the area, frustration etched on his face. He turns to the rest of. "See if you can spot any brass, anything that shows they were here."

We fan out, eyes scanning every inch of the rooftop. I crouch down, running my gloved hand over the concrete, feeling for shell casings, spent rounds, anything. But there's nothing. Not a single piece of brass, no weapons, no signs of blood. Just a few cigarette butts and the graffiti scrawled across one wall in jagged, angry strokes.

"What's that say?" Sergeant Cromer asks, squinting at the words.

Our interpreter steps forward, his face impassive as he reads the Arabic script.

"It says 'Death to America,'" he translates flatly.

It's not subtle, but it's effective, a reminder of where we stand.

"Real nice," Dubose mutters, giving the order to search for shell casings.

We fan out even more, but there's nothing – not a single piece of evidence the Muj were even here. It's like they've vanished into the shadows, leaving only scars on the concrete and walls.

I snort, feeling the irony settle over me. We're standing on a rooftop pocked with bullet holes, looking down at a city that wants us gone. And all we've got to show for it is a bit of paint on the wall.

Dubose glances around, irritation in his eyes. "Alright, boys, gather up," he says, his voice tight. "This was a dead end. Let's get back to the street."

As we regroup, my shoulders sag just a bit, the adrenaline fading. The guys exchange glances, muttering under their breath, a mix of frustration and disbelief. We poured through this building like a storm, and we've come up empty-handed.

Just as we reach the stairwell to descend, Dubose motions toward Archie and Hicks.

"Round up your guys. We're gonna hit that barbershop we passed on the way in."

Archie raises an eyebrow. "The one down the street, sarn't?"

"Yeah, that's the one," Dubose replies, sarcasm barely concealed in his voice. "Move it."

A bit of disappointment lingers as we file down the stairwell, cautious as ever. Just because we didn't meet resistance on the way up doesn't mean we're safe on the way down. Every step echoes off the narrow walls, the weight of the mission pressing down on us, even as we realize we've found nothing.

Once we reach the street, the burning car we passed earlier is still smoldering, its twisted metal casting eerie shadows against the walls. I don't know what I expected tonight, but tearing through an empty building to find nothing but a threat on a wall wasn't it.

As we make our way toward the barbershop, I can't help but glance over my shoulder, half-expecting to see the ghost of an enemy rifleman on that rooftop, watching us go.

Supposedly this barber shop has been flagged by intel as a potential weapons cache. We regroup, the adrenaline wearing off just enough to make the exhaustion start to creep in, but there's no time to rest. We file in a single line, pushing through the smoky, debris-strewn streets, until we spot the barbershop's faded sign hanging off its hinges. The shop itself is small, its glass door cracked, the sign dangling by one rusty bolt. The place looks like it hasn't seen a customer in quite some time, and every step closer has my stomach tightening, sensing this won't be the friendly trim-and-shave type of visit.

As we stack up outside, Dubose gives us the nod, and I'm the first through the door. My boots crunch against broken glass and dirt, and the smell inside is thick and stale, the lingering scent of cheap cologne mixing with the dust. The mirrors are cracked, their glass edges jagged, reflecting twisted images of ourselves as we move through. Patterson is right behind me, muttering under his breath, "Dude, this is someone's business. Can't we at least not wreck it?" I agree with the thought but know full well we're about to turn this place upside down.

Dubose's voice is low but firm, "Start searching – every drawer, every corner. If it can be lifted, lift it. We're looking for any hint of a weapons cache."

LT Chappell, meanwhile, does not share the same sentiment as Patterson and I do because he is straight up wrecking this place. There's no method to his madness; he's on his hands and knees, pounding on the floorboards with his fist, listening for hollow sounds. When he thinks he hears one, he grabs a nearby crowbar and pries up the floor, his face set with a kind of frantic determination. The rest of us watch for a second, torn between awe and disbelief, but we keep searching.

At one point, Patterson pulls open a drawer stuffed with razors and scissors, looking as if he's stumbled on a cache of IED making material but it's not. He lets out a huff, lifting the drawer up and dumping the contents on the floor, while Hicks rifles through a cupboard filled with old bottles of shampoo and disinfectant, each one clattering to the ground in a noisy pile.

Moret flips over a barber chair, revealing a stash of greasy towels tucked underneath. "Man, this doesn't feel like we're finding anything but someone's dirty laundry," he grumbles, shoving the chair aside.

LT Chappell is still tearing up the floor in a frenzy, sweat dripping down his face, ignoring the dirt caking his hands.

"We got intel this place is a hotbed for weapons. It's gotta be here somewhere!" he snaps, more to himself than to us.

He's pulling up floorboards now like a man possessed, exposing the shop's underfloor, which is nothing but sand and more sand. I can't tell if he's more frustrated or just embarrassed at how little we're finding.

After several more minutes of digging, it becomes painfully clear that this shop is just that – a barbershop. We came in, guns drawn, ready to find an armory, and all we've done is leave destruction in our wake. I can't help but feel a pang of guilt. Whoever owns this place is going to return to find their business in shambles, the floor half-torn up, chairs overturned, and glass everywhere. I would be so pissed if someone did this to my place of business.

Dubose glances over at Chappell, raising an eyebrow. "Sir, I think we're done here. Looks like this place doesn't have much beyond razors and hairspray."

Lieutenant Chappell, reluctantly, nods, and we start to file out. Patterson shakes his head as he steps over the mess we've made.

"So, we came in, wrecked the place, found absolutely jack, and now we're just... leaving?" He's half-laughing as he says it, but there's a hint of regret there too.

"Yep," I mutter, sharing the feeling. "This is grunt life, man. It doesn't have to make sense."

Back at the APC, we climb in, and as the doors close, Patterson and I exchange a glance, still baffled by the whirlwind of the last few minutes. We left someone's business in pieces and found nothing to show for it – just another bizarre chapter in a night filled with adrenaline, chaos, and the strange, unpredictable rhythms of war.

Chapter 3
The Camp is Burning
Early October 2004

It's early but the sun is up. The camp is quiet and there is nothing planned at the moment, a rare day of rest and Patterson and I are taking full advantage. We're lounging on our bunks, basking in the air conditioning and the rare luxury of a wall socket to charge our gear. The platoon's quarters are jammed with red bunk beds and personal junk piled wherever there's space. But compared to our last digs, this place is paradise. Our last "home" was barely standing—a cement skeleton with blown-out windows and crumbling walls, an open invitation for tetanus and tetanus's entire extended family. We slept in the hallway there, the only stretch of floor not completely buried in rubble. The place reeked of burn pits and spilled diesel, the stench riding every gust of hot wind. If an engineer were to look at that building, they'd be scratching their head, wondering how it hadn't collapsed yet. But now? I can't really begin to describe the total pile of shit it was. Now we have a building with walls, doors, and even AC. It felt almost...safe.

And then came the explosions. The familiar thud of mortars landing nearby breaks the silence, so ordinary now that it barely phases us. Patterson and I share a glance and smirk. Another day, another mortar. But then the scent of something sharper, something burning and dry, starts to fill the room. We smell it before we see it.

PFC Cassell bursts through the door, wide-eyed and shouting, "The camp's on fire!"

At first, I think he's joking, but the look on his face is dead serious. Patterson and I are up, grabbing what gear we can and sprinting toward the smoke already curling up from beyond the tents. When we reach the scene, I take one look at the flames and think, *No. Hell no.*

The fire is massive, flames taller than us tearing through the desert scrub, spreading like a wave of molten lava. The crackle of burning brush is so loud it drowns out the distant mortar blasts. And we're not equipped for this—armed only with shovels and our bare hands. I feel the heat before I even get close; it's like standing in front of an open furnace. My mind races as I try to make sense of this insanity.

Patterson slaps me on the back with that familiar, reckless grin. "Screw it! Let's dig some fire lines or pile dirt on it or something!"

It sounds ridiculous, but it's all we've got. With nothing but shovels, we dig into the dirt, slinging soil over the flames in some desperate attempt to hold them back. I can barely see with the smoke stinging my eyes, but I keep shoveling, breathing through my sleeve to avoid the thick, choking haze. The fire is an absolute beast, the flames tearing through the dry grass and thorny scrub like they're fuel, creeping closer with every second.

The rest of the platoon shows up, and I'm relieved to see our NCOs jumping into the fray. There's no time for "supervision" now. They're just as coated in sweat and dirt as the rest of us, sleeves rolled up, eyes squinted against the smoke. Even Moret is out here, wielding a pickax one-handed, his other arm completely useless in a bulky cast.

That cast has its own story, a reminder of our last mission out near Ramadi. We were moving at night, everything lit in that surreal green haze of night vision. No depth perception, just fuzzy outlines. We came across a set of railroad tracks with a drop on the other side.

Sergeant Hicks, bless him, warned us, but all he said was, "Small step, guys."

When I dropped down, I realized that "small step" was a solid three-foot drop. I managed to keep my footing, but I forgot to shout a warning back to Moret. He had the SAW, which made balancing almost impossible. I barely got two steps forward when I heard him crash to the ground, cursing loud enough to turn heads.

Hicks turned back, unimpressed. "You dumb motherfucker, I told you there was a step."

"You didn't say it was a three-foot drop! I think my wrist is broken!" Moret growled, clutching his arm.

"Shut up and keep moving," Hicks barked.

Moret sucked it up, even though his wrist was swelling by the minute. By the time we got back to camp, it looked like a balloon. He spent two days wrapped up with nothing but 100-mph tape, and sure enough, it turned out to be broken. Now I'm hauling his SAW until he heals. Every muscle in my arms hates me for it, but that's a problem for another day. Right now, we've got flames snapping at our heels.

The fire keeps advancing, an unstoppable force, with heat pounding down on us like a hammer. Each shovel of dirt feels pointless, but we dig in anyway. My lungs burn with every breath, my mouth filled with grit, and every infantryman—every "Joe"—is out here grinding away, half-blind from the smoke, faces set in that relentless, dogged determination you only see when people are pushed to their limits. We're in the furnace now, and strangely, there's a raw exhilaration in it. We're knee-deep in smoke, steel to earth, battling this inferno back one shovel of dirt at a time.

We have no backup; there's no 911 to call, no fire trucks rushing in with hoses and water. We are the rescue. And Joe—Joe doesn't know when to quit. Each of us digs with pure, unrelenting will, refusing to let this monster swallow the camp. Finally, through God's grace and sheer grit, we start to gain ground. The flames slowly retreat, and somehow, against all odds, we're winning this fight. I don't believe it.

Patterson keeps yelling out over the roar of the flames, trying to rally the rest of us. "Keep it up! Don't let this bastard win!"

We're sweating, coughing, digging like madmen, and still the fire pushes forward. The flames are inches away from the motor pool now, the heat radiating off them like a wall. If it reaches our trucks, we're looking at an inferno that'll take everything. I glance over at Moret, who's still swinging that pickax one-handed, his face clenched with the effort.

For every inch we manage to push the flames back, they creep forward by two. It's a brutal, exhausting stalemate. I can feel the sweat pouring down my face, my whole body straining with each shovelful of dirt. We dig deeper, faster, praying that we can cut a fire line wide enough to stop the spread. My arms are numb, my eyes sting, and the fire just keeps coming. But quitting isn't an option. We're out here on our own, and either we stop this fire, or we lose the camp.

Joe's still grinding away, shoveling dirt with a fury we didn't know we had. Smoke fills the air, so thick I can barely see Patterson a few feet away. My lungs are on fire, each breath feels like sandpaper, but we keep going, one shovel of dirt at a time.

And then, slowly—miraculously—the flames start to die down. I don't believe it at first. It seems impossible, but we've actually done it. The fire's retreating, the smoke beginning to thin. Patterson lets out a cheer, slapping me on the back, his face covered in soot and sweat.

"Can you believe this, man?" I gasp, coughing and laughing all at once.

Someone mutters something about an AAM, an Army Achievement Medal, and we all laugh, the sound hollow but filled with relief. By the end of this deployment, this insane day will probably be forgotten. But we'll remember. As I catch my breath and look out over the smoldering field, I know this one's going in my journal.

Chapter 4

Combat Outpost - Everyone is on Fire

Early November 2004

Camp Habbaniyah is now a distant memory. Sure, it's only been about three days, but time doesn't flow normally here at Combat Outpost. Out here, a minute can stretch forever in the baking sun or snap to nothing in a flash of danger. The basics are stripped to the bone—no showers, no chow hall, and definitely no air conditioning. Bunk beds are the one concession to "comfort," if you could call them that: hard red metal frames, stacked tight in windowless rooms where the air sits hot and thick, untouched by a breeze. Doors are optional here, just more stuff to get blown off or broken anyway.

Haji used to come by in his battered truck to service the port-a-johns, a necessary but despised task. He did it faithfully until one day he was yanked from his truck and murdered in broad daylight for the crime of helping U.S. troops. Now we burn our own waste in makeshift barrels, marines and soldiers alike, stirring the stinking mix as it burns to keep it from solidifying at the bottom. Another surreal aspect of a surreal life.

Combat Outpost—COP—is little more than a scattering of battered buildings, half of them speckled with bullet holes or scarred from shrapnel and indirect fire. The whole place measures roughly 600 by 1,200 feet, just north of Route Michigan on the eastern side of Ramadi. One saving grace here? It's far from the flagpole, away from the bureaucratic military garrison crap. At the bigger bases, officers lose their minds if you miss a salute. But here, nobody cares about rank pomp and ceremony. It's no-salute territory, and no one's worried about how crisp your uniform is. We're too busy trying to survive.

We rolled out from Habbaniyah late last night, driving in a blackout convoy under cover of darkness. The 40-minute trip felt like an hour as we navigated blind turns and swerved around barrier posts that seemed to jump into the road. At one point, I nearly put our Humvee into a concrete wall.

"Damn, Stokes! Good driving!" Sergeant Dubose shouted.

I caught my breath and muttered, "What the hell was that?"

"A barrier of some sort. Keep an eye out; we're getting close," he replied. Dubose's accent was pure country—more "backwoods" than "Southern gentleman."

He was from Florida and was happiest talking about hunting or fishing, stuff that couldn't be further from here. Driving with night vision goggles at highway speeds? Probably as insane as it sounds, but somehow, we made it. Our LT, platoon sergeant, and a few squad leaders have been out doing "right seat rides" with the marines we're replacing. It's a tradition—new leadership rides along with the outgoing unit to get a feel for the terrain, picking up tips on hotspots and dangerous routes. I overheard some of our guys talking about the marines' shoot-first approach.

"If they even think they see something sketchy, they'll light it up," one of them said. "One shot, and the whole platoon starts firing like hell. They don't give a damn."

It sounded reckless, but Ramadi had already shown us it wasn't a place for second chances. These marines had been here longer than I have been an infantryman. They appeared tired but fierce, as if they'd crawled out of hell itself, with dirt caked into every crevice and eyes that carried a wild intensity. It was a question I'd have to wait to answer: *Was this our future?* For now, I was ready to kick in more doors, and I couldn't wait to get started.

Everyone is on Fire

Combat Outpost sits quietly under the hot, unrelenting sun, its perimeter guarded by fortified fighting positions manned by two soldiers each. It's midday, and first squad is just coming off our tower guard shift. Every post reports to the SOG—Sergeant on Guard—a steady fixture who keeps tabs on everything. Sergeant Archie came off his post with a warning: there was a lone Iraqi cop near the roundabout. Iraqi police rarely worked solo, so it raised red flags. Archie told the next shift to keep an eye on him, but higher-ups weren't overly concerned, and orders came down to "just observe."

On this day, Private First Class Saffel and Private First Class Deeley now have the tower overlooking the intersection at Route Michigan and Route Nova. In the midst of an otherwise uneventful shift, they see the Iraqi police car that Sergeant Archie mentioned parked dead center in the roundabout, its lights blinking in the sun. The fact Iraqi police usually work in pairs, and this one is solo officer really is a cause for concern.

Saffel radios up to the SOG, asking if the police are supposed to be helping with the convoy that's en route to the base. The answer comes back sharp and certain: no. Saffel relays that the car is sitting suspiciously in the intersection, but the orders are clear—no action, just observe. Deeley has his 240B machine gun trained on the car, finger tense on the trigger, his instincts firing up. He mutters, "This doesn't feel right; we've got to do something." But orders are orders, and all they can do is wait.

Just three minutes out, the convoy is closing in, a 7-ton truck packed with half of Charlie Company's third platoon. Saffel breaks protocol slightly, warning the gate guard to stand ready, just in case. As the truck approaches, the lone officer abandons his traffic directing, climbs back into his patrol car, and waits. In an instant, the car launches forward, ramming the side of the 7-ton, and detonates. The blast is deafening, a massive wall of fire and metal that ripples through the intersection, sending shockwaves up to the tower. Saffel and Deeley watch in horror as the scene unfolds. Soldiers inside the truck scramble to escape, their clothes and gear melting in the inferno, while the convoy returns fire, fearing a full ambush.

In the chaos, Saffel yells out, "IED, IED!" before he realizes the bomb wasn't buried. "VBIED, VBIED!" he corrects, trying to signal to anyone who can hear. A Vehicle-Borne Improvised Explosive Device (VBIED) is an IED concealed in a vehicle, turning it into a mobile bomb, or car bomb as they are routinely called. Often used in ambushes or suicide attacks, VBIEDs deliver massive explosions capable of leveling buildings and obliterating armored convoys.

Just as the smoke settles, their Sergeant on Guard storms into the tower. Without a word, he rips off their helmets, swinging at them in rage. "This isn't my fault," he spits, seething with fury. "You two are going down before I do."

When the dust finally settles, about seventeen soldiers are injured, three of them critically and may not make it. Orders to "just observe" had left them powerless, but the fallout comes down on Saffel and Deeley, a burden that, in time, will haunt them both. Higher command drags the Sergeant on Guard from the tower, but the damage is done. Deeley is reassigned to Charlie company, filling in for the wounded in third platoon. Saffel, left with the bitter memory, can barely stomach his machine gun again and refuses to ever work again under the Sergeant on Guard that day.

Years later, the guilt remains, deeply rooted in the memories of those days. Ten years of psychiatric care hasn't quieted the pain of knowing they could have saved soldiers from injury had they been allowed to act. Following orders seemed the right choice then, but time has shown just how heavy that choice would weigh. Combat is brutal and people get hurt.

Chapter 5

Sweat and Gunfire

November 10th, 2004

Today, we're setting up an Entry Control Point (ECP) in the northeastern part of Ramadi, along Route Apple in the Al Sofia district. It's positioned north of Combat Outpost, south of the Euphrates River. The sun's barely up, and we're already at it—Joe is out here with his hands wrapped around concertina wire, pulling it across the rough road, his gloves torn and hands bleeding from the thorns and sharp rubble. This is no easy job. The wire snags on every bit of rock and brush it can find, like it's actively fighting back.

Half of us are wrestling with the ECP setup, dragging metal barriers and setting up sandbags. The rest are spread out, pulling security with eyes glued to the horizon. Gunners are locked and loaded on top of the Humvees, and Joes are interspersed in a defensive 360-degree perimeter. The river to the north may keep our backs somewhat safe, but we don't have the luxury of assuming it's clear. To the south, we catch faint gunshots echoing from the city, popping off like distant firecrackers, a grim reminder that our day's about to heat up. It's going to be a two- or three-day mission, meaning we're out here in Ramadi's backyard without relief. Sleeping in Humvees tonight is already feeling inevitable.

After about an hour, the checkpoint's set up and running smoothly. Vehicles approach cautiously, headlights flickering as we signal them forward. The drivers' faces are tense, and I don't blame them. They've got no idea what's waiting in the roadblocks ahead. Each car is stopped, searched, and sent through with efficient rhythm.

Just as I start to think things might go without a hitch, the infantry gods laugh in our faces. An rocket whistles through the air, trailing a streak of smoke as it flies low over our ECP, missing us by mere feet. Instinctively, we all hit the dirt in perfect unison.Schuh, manning the 240, snaps up.

"Sergeant Cromer, I saw where that came from!"

Cromer's reply is instant, barking orders with zero hesitation. "Well, shoot the motherfuckers!"

Schuh opens fire, the 240 thundering as he sends a rain of rounds across the river. The rest of us aren't about to let him have all the fun—we let loose, turning north and unloading in a near-symphony of gunfire. The sound is deafening, and I'm emptying my mag like it's my last. There's no such thing as overkill in Ramadi; every one of us pulls that trigger like the devil himself is breathing down our necks. We're all facing north, momentarily forgetting both flanks and our six. Tactics be damned. Right now, it's a race to see who can pull their trigger the fastest. I didn't win, but I certainly didn't lose.

In seconds, our ECP is in tatters, and so is our plan. Cromer calls out, "Alright, pack it up! We're rolling out!" The gunfire from the south is getting louder, and that last AK shot was close enough to feel.

"Let's go, boys, keep pulling security!" the LT adds.

"Man, we just set this thing up," I grumble to Moret, flexing my hands in frustration and looking at my shredded gloves. "These gloves are all kinds of messed up."

Moret just shrugs. "Yeah, but we just got shot at, so there's that."

"Fair point."

We shove the concertina wire back onto the trucks, hands still bleeding, sweat stinging our cuts. The Humvees crawl forward beside us as we dismount, maneuvering on foot toward the gunfire. Ahead of us lies a swath of land covered in dirt mounds, overgrown vegetation, and scattered outbuildings. It's the ideal hiding place for insurgents. Perfectly shitty terrain to cross.

The sharp crack of an AK-47 erupts from behind one of the mounds, and my adrenaline spikes. It's close, so close I can almost feel the vibrations in my chest. But the vegetation's too thick to see where exactly it came from.

"Return fire!" the LT shouts from behind first squad.

Not waiting for another order, I drop to a knee behind a mound, steady my rifle, and start firing. The rest of the squad follows, sending bursts of gunfire into the bushes. Sergeant Archie fires a 40mm high-explosive round from his M203 grenade launcher. The air shakes with the dull thud of the explosion. Overhead, and only a few blocks over, two Cobra gunships are sweeping in, and, like avenging angels, they rain rockets and bullets on the fighters below, ripping through the date fields. The insurgents are crazy enough to be shooting at them with AKs, bullets pinging uselessly off the Cobras' armor, if even hitting them at all.

We're advancing now, bounding forward in textbook fireteam formation—one team suppresses while the other moves. It's exactly what we drilled back in basic training. I got to be honest though, I can't believe we are actually doing this. I assumed in an urban environment there wouldn't be room for this type of tactic but here we are, textbook bounding overwatch.Here though, it's life and death. I glance to the east. Another squad moves in sync with us, using the Humvees as cover. They pass by the bodies of three beheaded Iraqi policemen, flies swarming, the stench indescribable. A reminder of the brutality lurking everywhere in this city. From the turret, Schuh lets off another burst, only to obliterate a scarecrow. Straw bursts into the air, giving us a brief, absurd laugh in the middle of the madness. Even out here, in the dirt and blood, we can still find something to laugh about.

My team reaches a small outbuilding, and I'm itching to kick the door in. This is my moment. Every infantryman dreams of a breach. With a hard kick, I hit the door, but it doesn't budge. Again, nothing. My breathing's heavy; I'm exhausted but too stubborn to give up. One last heave with my shoulder, and the door creaks open. I sweep the room with my rifle, only to find an empty shed, a lone garden hose the only "enemy" inside. I laugh, but frustration gnaws at me. Big badass Private First Class Stokely just breached and cleared the American equivalent of a backyard lawn mower shed. The garden hose on the ground has no idea how lucky it is that it's not a terrorist. There's no glory here, only gritty reality.

We move again, pressing closer to the houses. The insurgents are close enough now that we can hear them yelling in Arabic. LT Chappell, who can speak Arabic quite well, can barely make out what they're saying over the roar of the Cobras still strafing the area.

Finally, the LT orders us onto a rooftop. After clearing the house below, we take positions up top. I scan

41

the horizon through my ACOG optic, every movement in the alley below sending a ripple of tension through me. About 200 meters out, I see three men in black ski masks sprint across the alley, vaulting a fence. They're unarmed, but in Ramadi, that means nothing. I hesitate, and the moment's gone. I report it to my squad leader, who calls it in, but I'm left wondering if I missed my chance to stop something bigger.

Sergeant Dubose moves up next to me, and, as if we're back on base, he says, "You think Clark and Lana are gonna get together?"

I smirk, momentarily distracted from the insanity around us. "I don't know, man. Lois is in the picture now, right?" Smallville has become our favorite show to watch and talk about.

More gunfire interrupts us, but he just shakes his head.

"Yeah, but something's gotta happen with him and Lana, right?"

"God, I hope so."

Bursts of AK-47 fire break out nearby, closer this time. Our truck gunners return fire, but no hits. Over on another rooftop, Bronstad and Lineweber play a deadly game of whack-a-mole, taking turns popping up from behind cover. Then, to their utter disbelief, the homeowner crawls out with a tray of tea and cookies. In the middle of a firefight, albeit mild, this man is calmly offering hospitality.

"These are delicious," Bronstad says, almost in awe.

It's absurd, yet somehow fitting for this insane place. In Ramadi, you have three kinds of people: those who are grateful we're here, those who are sick of us, and those who want us gone by any means necessary. For some, we're liberators. For others, we're another occupation. It's a complicated mess, but none of that matters to me. Right now, I'm just a 19-year-old infantryman trying to survive the day.

By now, the platoon has finished whatever we were out here to do, and we're ordered back to the trucks. We've spent so much of this deployment going back and forth between mounted and dismounted missions. In South Korea, we were light infantry through and through—on foot for every mile, our bread and butter. Technically, we're air assault, but rarely did we see the inside of a chopper except in training. Iraq's different. Here, we're mounted half the time, rotating squads to drive and man the turrets, while the others dismount and handle the dirty work. It's not what we're used to, but at this point, there's no real "usual." We adjust and do the job.

Once loaded up, we head for the next objective: clearing and searching a cluster of houses in a nearby neighborhood. Over the radio, we hear that one of our sister companies had a platoon leader take a round to the head—probably a sniper. He's still alive, last they heard, and it'll be a miracle if he makes it.

We roll into the neighborhood on the edge of town. It's a mix of narrow courtyards and high gates, each house nearly identical in design. The smell hits us first—a nasty blend of diesel, sewage, and dust. It's the kind of stench you never quite get used to. My squad fans out around the Humvees, setting up security while 2nd Squad starts the search. Several of the Humvees are lined along a road that runs the length of the neighborhood. Palm trees are scattered along both sides, half-hidden by thick vegetation, and a shallow ditch follows the road, filled with stagnant water.

I start pacing between the Humvees, scanning the surroundings. That's when I hear it—a high-pitched zip cutting through the air right past my ear. My body drops instantly, hitting the ground before I even register what happened. My heart's racing, and I'm lying there, hoping I didn't just piss my pants.

That was a sniper shot, no question about it. I glance over at the guys nearby, expecting to see alarm in their faces, but they're just looking at me, confused. They didn't hear it. Hell, nobody heard it but me. That sniper round missed me by inches, and no one knows it but me, the shooter, and the Lord above.

I report it to my team leader, but he just shrugs it off. Probably because 1st Platoon found a huge stash of rifles, rockets, and mortars that we're now tasked with loading up. So much for a near-death experience. Guess that bullet didn't count unless it connected.

"A platoon leader just got sniped in the head like an hour ago," I mutter under my breath, "but sure, let's all act like that shot wasn't close."

As we load up, I grumble to myself for the hundredth time, "I should've joined the Air Force." But deep down, I know I wouldn't fit anywhere else, not really. Here, in the dust and chaos, this hellish corner of Ramadi is somehow where I'm meant to be.

Chapter 6

The Gauntlet

November 12th, 2004

The day starts like any other: a simple supply run to Camp Ramadi, also known as Junction City—or just JC. It's typically a smooth, 20-minute drive to the west side of the city. But our unit's home base, Combat Outpost, sits on the eastern edge of Ramadi, so we usually play it safe, looping around Habbaniyah Lake to avoid the city itself. Today, though, we're taking the short route. Up until now, our platoon has been lucky; three months in-country without a single hit from an improvised explosive device. We'd heard all the briefings about IEDs, especially here in Anbar Province, but I'm beginning to wonder if the danger's been overhyped. But today is about to show me just how naive that thought really is.

"Stoke! Get the Humvee pulled around so we can load our gear," Sergeant Dubose yells over the rumble of engines firing up. "We're two Humvees behind the seven-ton."

"Roger that, Sergeant!"

Private First Class Bapst, a saw gunner from third squad, helps load up our gear before climbing up to man the .50. Bapst is like a cowboy straight out of an old Western—polite, soft-spoken, and every bit the gentleman. He's even got a Stetson hat back home to prove it. Sergeant Dubose hops into the passenger seat, cradling his last Dr. Pepper.

"We need to stock up on these while we're at JC," he grins, shaking the can.

"Definitely!" I say, chuckling.

Even though sergeants and privates aren't supposed to get too friendly, Sergeant Dubose and I have a solid bond, the kind you only get from shared grit and grueling training. He'll still chew me out if I mess up, though; one misstep during a training op in Korea taught me that the hard way. I'd skipped filling my water the night before, figuring I'd do it in the morning, and he made me low-crawl a full football field in full kit—just to drive the lesson home. By the end, I was half-dead, but I never slacked on water again.

Our convoy pulls out through the gate and turns right onto Route Michigan, a main artery running through Ramadi. Known as one of the most dangerous roads in the world, it's seen more than its share of explosions. As we move into Marine-controlled territory, we hop the center median to clear a path, our .50-cals trained on anyone slow to yield. For now, the streets are bustling, locals going about their day as if oblivious to the heavy U.S. presence. And then it all changes.

An IED detonates on my side of the Humvee just as we cross a busy intersection. The shockwave rattles the armor, and for a split second, I worry about Bapst, who's more exposed up in the turret.

"Bapst! You good?" I shout, straining to be heard.

"Just keep driving, Stoke!" Dubose commands, his voice cutting through the adrenaline.

"I'm good!" Bapst replies, one knuckle bleeding from a graze of shrapnel.

The explosion was jarring, but we're all okay, and the convoy rolls on. With the excitement and relief surging through us, we can't help but feel pumped. We just took an IED hit—and we're still rolling.

Once inside the gates at Camp Ramadi, we go through the usual ritual: magazines out, rifles cleared. This isn't the way we do it at Combat Outpost. There, we keep our weapons loaded 24/7—taking them apart to clean is the closest we come to "unloaded." I once saw Bowden accidentally shoot a round from his bunk while doing a function check. The round killed the squad's fridge. It was hilarious, though it sounded like a full RPG hit when it happened.

After clearing our weapons, we inspect the Humvee. There's shrapnel embedded in the side, small craters in the armor, but nothing catastrophic. We're stoked. Dr. Pepper and snacks await at the PX, and there's a chow hall we're dying to check out. But when some of our guys head in for food, the Fobbits—the guys who rarely leave the base—turn them away because they're too dirty.

"Fuck those guys," a squadleader grumbles.

These guys sit in a cushy world where clean uniforms and hot meals are guaranteed. We practically live outside the wire, our uniforms filthy, our weapons loaded, and our bodies covered in sweat and grime. Fobbits will never get it.

As we load up for the ride back, we do something we'd never normally do: take the same route twice in one day. It's risky and goes against doctrine, but we're aiming for speed, not safety. The road winds tightly, twisting and curving, flanked by mounds of dirt, rubble, and trash piled high along each side. This is where insurgents thrive—setting bombs where we can't see them until it's too late.

About halfway back to Combat Outpost, the first explosion erupts without warning, feet from the front of our Humvee. A roaring blast, and the world goes dark as debris rains down, clanging against the armor like hailstones. I grip the wheel tighter, squinting through the dust cloud, and try to keep us steady. Day has turned into night in only a moment.

"I can't see, Sergeant!" I yell.

"Just keep fucking driving!" Sergeant Dubose shouts back, his tone as steely as ever.

I hit the gas and swerve, struggling to keep the Humvee on the road as pieces of jagged metal bounce off the sides. Then, just as we break through the cloud, a second blast detonates on the passenger side. A hot wave of pressure slams into us, jarring my vision. The shockwave hits like a punch to the chest, vibrating through the metal, and I feel the heat clawing its way into the vehicle.

"Shit, another one!" someone yells from the back!

Everything is shaking. My hands are white-knuckled, gripping the steering wheel as we surge forward. Each IED detonating feels like a fist coming down, slamming into the truck's armor, rocking us from side to side. Inside, it's a storm of rattling metal, dust, and adrenaline. The force jars every nerve, every bone, leaving my heart pounding in my throat.

"Just keep moving, Stoke!" Dubose's voice breaks through the chaos, urgent and demanding.

His words anchor me, and I push down harder on the gas, careening forward through the shifting cloud of dust and smoke.

For seconds that feel like hours, we are blind, enveloped in a cloud so thick it's like night. The road is gone, visibility is zero, and all I can do is trust my memory of the curves ahead and my gut, praying nothing blocks our path. And then, just as my heart finds some semblance of rhythm, the road ahead clears.

But the relief doesn't last. A fourth explosion erupts two Humvee in front of us, and this time, the blast is strong enough to lift the vehicle's back tires off the ground. I swerve, barely avoiding the fragments shooting through the air. Inside our vehicle, silence falls—a tense, terrified quiet where I know we're all thinking the same thing: How many more are there?

We finally made it back and I've never been so relieved to pull back into Combat Outpost. As we roll through the gate, the gunners clear only the weapons mounted on the trucks. The rifles we carry? Those stay loaded. Sergeant Dubose directs me to park the Humvee over by the maintenance bay near where the QRF beds down so we can unload and check out the damage to the vehicle. As soon as we're parked, Bapst and I start sharing our war story with anyone who'll listen, hyped on adrenaline and a good dose of disbelief.

"We're some badass motherfuckers," I think as we finally settle down a bit.

Usually, thoughts like that don't come up when you're in the thick of it—they have to wait until you're back inside the wire where there's room for bravado. And this time, there's no need for exaggeration.

YellowHammer glances over at me and tells me to hold out my hands. They're still shaking, sure enough, but we're all in one piece, and I can feel my nerves steadying. Across from me, though, the other passenger—a team leader from another squad, a little older, married with kids—is sitting rigid. He doesn't move at first, not even to climb out of the truck. He's just... processing it all. We went three months without a single IED, and today, we hit four, three of them against this truck alone.

"You guys okay?" Sergeant Dubose asks, looking us over.

"We're good, but he doesn't look it," I say, nodding toward the team leader.

"He'll be fine; just give him a minute," Dubose replies. "Now get this stuff unloaded and relax for a bit."

"Roger that, Sergeant," I answer, finally letting myself feel the relief settle in.

Chapter 7

They Almost Got Us Sergeant

November 14th, 2004

It's been eight days since that VBIED tore through Charlie Company, 3rd Platoon. In seconds, they were combat ineffective, just...gone. If it could happen to them, it could happen to any of us. When we got the word that we'd be loading into the same 7-ton trucks, I felt that twist in my stomach. Not the regular pre-mission nerves, either—the kind that you bury down deep so no one sees it.

Every time we leave the wire, it's like clockwork: contact. Two days back, I heard that bone-chilling call for a medic through the bursts of gunfire for the first time. I dropped to a knee, rifle steady, staring down a dusty alley that reeked like burning trash. The kneeling did two things—kept me low, a smaller target, and let me gulp water in the 120-degree heat, just to stay functional. The air here feels thick with something I can't put into words, almost like the tension you feel right before a storm.

Behind me, our LT's truck was parked near a grain shop and right next to a snack shop. I could smell the food through the heat, and my stomach rumbled despite myself. Inside, LT, Sergeant Dubose, and Sweeney were hunched over, heads together, talking about a 60mm mortar tube they found nearby, deciding how to handle questioning the locals.

I was just there, pulling security and minding my own, when a few Muj fighters thought it'd be a good time to throw some automatic fire our way. It wasn't even from the alley I was watching, so I just stayed steady, waiting for our gunners to handle it. Sure enough, the .50 cal barked back, and that deep, comforting rhythm of return fire rolled out. But then I heard the hiss of an RPG in the air, and my pulse kicked up a notch. RPGs—they're wildly inaccurate, but when they connect, it's ugly. Picture a Nerf football with fins but one that can turn you to pieces if it lands right.

In that moment, I saw Robinson cartwheel out of the street like something out of a damn movie. The RPG skipped, ricocheting off the ground, missing him, then bounced off a Humvee tire, and clipped Staff Sergeant McInnis's leg. Mac hit the ground in a somersault, clutching his leg, cursing up a storm.

Close by, the sniper was facing the wrong way, and Sikonia yelled, "Hey, man, turn the fuck around!"

The sniper swung around just as someone screamed, "Medic! Mac is hit!"

Doc Meyer was there within seconds, calm and efficient, as if he'd done this a thousand times. He checked Mac over, determined it was probably a hairline fracture, and a few days later, Mac was back in the fight.

Now, though, we're heading back into Indian country. My stomach knots as I hoist myself into the back of the 7-ton, feeling every inch of the weight on my shoulders. I sink into the middle seat, close my eyes for a second, and say my usual prayer. It's routine now—words I hold onto every time we leave the wire because guys get hit here regularly, and I'm not naive enough to think luck lasts forever.

With the rest of the platoon loaded, the 7-ton grumbles to life, rattling and growling as it pulls forward. The diesel fumes hit harder back here, thick in the air, filling my nose and lungs, like the prelude to the tension of every mission. It's the kind of smell that clings to you, along with the dust, grit, and heat of Ramadi.

We roll through the gate, heading west down Route Michigan. A few minutes in, we hit the roundabout and angle southwest into RPG Alley, a stretch of road whose name is too damn on-the-nose to be funny. Whoever labeled it had a dark sense of humor. Every bump and rattle of the 7-ton feels amplified, and the seconds stretch as we bounce over medians, barely giving them a second thought. We're close to the AO now, the point where we'll jump out into the street. The squad leader's voice cuts through the engine noise, "Get ready for dismount!"

I reach for my rifle, instinct kicking in as my thumb checks the selector switch. Safe. I always double-check, even though it's automatic by now—another lesson drilled in deep. I'll never forget the tongue-lashing I got in basic for skipping that step. The drill sergeant made me write a two-page letter to my battle buddy's "parents," apologizing for "killing" their son with my unsafe weapon. That kind of humiliation sticks with you. My rifle stays on safe, even as my boots thud onto the pavement.

As we spill out onto the street, my team leader points me toward my security post. I nod, lowering to one knee, taking in the world around me. Today, our alert levels are already through the roof—word came through the radios about two separate suicide bombers hitting Marine positions nearby. We're all on edge, every sense turned up, hyper-focused on any movement, any flash of metal, any sign that something isn't right.

Five minutes pass. The trucks have rumbled off, and we're waiting for orders to move. I stay low, shifting on my knee, still scanning my sector when, out of nowhere, a guy in a black ski mask strolls out of an alley about 200 meters down, like he owns the place. And he isn't trying to be stealthy at all, just walking. My rifle's in my shoulder in a second, ACOG leveled, the bead on his chest. No weapon in his hands—what the hell is this guy doing?

Then I spot them: soldiers from another company trailing behind him, all in full gear. It clicks; he's their interpreter. I lower my rifle a hair, but the thought won't leave my head—why the hell would they put him up front? He had no idea how close he was to getting smoked. I'm dead sure half the guys in my platoon wouldn't have hesitated.

I shake my head, letting out a long breath I didn't realize I was holding. If things had gone differently, I'd be explaining to command right now why I thought another company no longer needed their interpreter.

"Stoke, let's go!" Sergeant Hicks shouts, snapping me back.

I rise, shifting my rifle as I move back toward the platoon, bracing myself for whatever comes next.I shuffle back to the platoon, joining the staggered column as we move down the street. It's our go-to formation in these neighborhoods, giving us eyes on every corner and side street, keeping us spaced out in case an IED blows or gunfire erupts.

The streets have gotten quieter over the past 20 minutes, and my senses are on high alert. I'm near the middle of the column when the first quarter of the platoon turns down a side street. Up ahead, PFC Bapst from third squad is leading on the left side with Corporal Janusz opposite him on the right. Behind Bapst are PFC Bronstad and Sweeney. Just as I'm about to round the corner, gunfire cracks through the air. It's sudden, violent, and relentless—a spray-and-pray tactic that sends rounds scattering everywhere as an insurgent swings his AK-47 from around a corner.

Bapst is frozen for a second as bullets stitch the dirt around him and ricochet off walls. It feels like slow motion as he watches them punch into the ground and miraculously miss him entirely.

"Bapst! Get the fuck down!" Janusz yells, but Bapst doesn't flinch.

Instead, he plants his feet, shoulders his M249, and lets loose on the corner where the shooter is hiding. Sweeney, a few paces back, raises his own M249 to join in, but his weapon jams—a belt override. He's frantically trying to clear it as rounds chew up the dirt around him.

Bronstad, behind them, shoulders his M4, squeezes off a few rounds, and drops behind a blue bongo truck for cover. Then an enemy round skips off a pile of scrap in front of him, ricocheting into his lower back. He takes the hit, going down, while Sweeney—likely saved by Bronstad's bad luck—keeps wrestling with his jammed weapon.

As more of us open fire, we gain the upper hand. The insurgent slips back behind cover, leaving nothing but the blood splattered across the corner as his buddies haul him away.

"I'm hit!" Bronstad shouts, struggling to stay upright.

Sweeney, still clearing his weapon, doesn't hear him at first.

"Yo, I'm fucking hit!" Bronstad yells again.

"What?" Sweeney looks over, then realizes what happened. "Oh, shit! Medic! Bronstad's hit!"

They pull Bronstad back into a nearby courtyard, and he's trying to stay calm until his team leader starts panicking.

"Holy shit! You're fucking shot, Bronstad!"

Rule one when treating a wounded soldier: stay calm. But his team-leader's freakout isn't doing Bronstad any favors. And the Yellow Jackets Bronstad downs before every mission aren't helping either. The guy's been popping those ephedra-packed stimulants like candy for weeks. I'm pretty sure they're illegal, and now it's clear why he can never sleep. Late at night, I'd pass his bunk and hear him talking to himself about how he can't eat, can't sleep, feels jacked up all the time.

Several houses back, Doc Meyer hears the call for a medic and sprints to the courtyard, no regard for the potential danger. Admirable, if not downright dangerous—I'm afraid one day he'll get hurt moving like that. Once beside Bronstad, Doc Meyer gets to work, kneeling at his side, unfazed by the blood or panic.

"How bad is it, Doc?" Bronstad asks, his voice catching.

"Hold still, man!" Doc cuts his pants open, assessing the wound.

As I walk past, I catch a glimpse of Bronstad face-down, ass-up, and Doc working steadily. Bronstad looks pale, scared shitless but stable.

"Doc, be straight with me. How bad is it?" Bronstad's voice rises, shaking. He's asking people to tell his mom he loves her if he doesn't make it.

"Listen, it didn't hit anything vital. You're going to be fine, okay?" Doc says calmly.

"I don't wanna die, First Sergeant!" Bronstad cries as First Sergeant Adams kneels down next to him.

The First Sergeant, always out here with us, puts a hand on his shoulder and speaks in a fatherly tone, telling him he's going to be fine. Bronstad settles, breathing slower as Doc Meyer and Adams talk him down.

Bronstad's CASEVACed back to Combat Outpost, and we regroup, continuing the patrol. CASEVAC (Casualty Evacuation) is the rapid transport of wounded personnel from the battlefield using any available vehicle, often under fire and without dedicated medical teams. Unlike MEDEVAC, it lacks formal medical support and Geneva Convention protections, prioritizing speed over resources. Apart from that firefight, it's been a quiet day, but that adrenaline spike has me on high alert now, eyes scanning the road ahead, listening to the silence that never feels right in this place.

The streets are quiet now, and it's my turn to cross the intersection. Halfway across, I spot a white and orange car rolling toward me from about 200 meters out. Maybe the driver hasn't seen me yet. I'll give him a second to adjust. Civilians here know not to approach us unless they're waved through or passing a checkpoint.

I wave a hand around to get the driver's attention but I don't think he sees me. I then raise one hand, in a "halting' position, and with the other, I keep waving. Nothing. I shout, trying to get through, but the car keeps coming, now about 150 meters away. The VBIED that hit a Marine group this morning flashes in my mind—this could

57

be another suicide bomber. At 100 meters, the car is still moving, steady, determined.

I bring up my rifle, settling the red dot of my M68 on the driver's chest just above the wheel. Sergeant Dubose swapped my ACOG for himself recently, so I'm back to the red dot, but at this range, it'll do the job. I can see his face now—no hesitation, no fear. He's 50 meters out, and my thumb flicks the selector switch from safe to semi as I squeeze the trigger.

The rifle fires, shots ringing out, and I am a bit startled because Schuh, just a few yards to my left, is already in on the action. He sees the car ignoring my every command to stop, and he's got an M240 on him, bipod knocked off during that last firefight when Bronstad got hit. He keeps his finger pressed, sending a heavy stream of rounds into the car, and right as my rifle jams after seven shots, the vehicle jerks off course. The driver is hit—"ventilated" would be a better word—but the car keeps rolling. There's no guarantee this threat is over. Insurgents sometimes rig cars to blow with a remote, driver or no driver, so I pull back, bolting for the wall behind me, pressing up against it, ears covered. This thing could go up any second. But nothing happens.

I clear the jam, mentally kicking myself for not cleaning my weapon more often, then peek around the corner. Schuh's still standing there, completely unfazed, machine gun lowered like it's just another day.

"Holy shit, Schuh!" Mullins yells, wide-eyed. "What the fuck was that?"

Schuh just shrugs, barely looking back. He later tells me he'd made peace with it—either he'd die, or he wouldn't.

The car is a smoldering heap now, bullet-riddled, engine smoking. The driver, slumped over, isn't going anywhere. We certainly aren't going to waste time checking it so we keep moving forward. Here in Ramadi, the rules of engagement are straightforward: a vehicle charging us and failing to stop is considered hostile. No doubts, no hesitations.

A few blocks later, I'm jolted by another blast of machine gun fire. It's so close I duck out of reflex. When I turn, I realize it's one of our guys. YellowHammer's out in the middle of an intersection, M249 squared up against his shoulder, unloading on a car that sped toward him. It's the same thing Schuh and I just went through—a potential VBIED barreling toward us, ignoring every warning, every chance to stop.

We don't even bother searching the car or the driver. If it's a VBIED, there's no need to get close—it could blow any second. So we march on, eyes forward, weapons ready, another potential blast left smoldering in the street behind us.

The sun is setting as we reach our AO for the night, casting a murky orange glow over the neighborhood. We've spent the entire day combing through streets and houses, moving room by room, a steady rhythm of kicks and knocks, checks and searches. During one search, I knelt to check a ground-level cabinet and found a small black wooden box stashed beneath a pile of blankets. Curiosity took over. I pulled it out, opened it, and blinked hard—a stack of U.S. cash, nearly 15 grand by my count. For a 19-year-old, that's a fortune. The thought crossed my mind: how and why did the homeowner stash this pile of cash here? But there's no rule against it, so I put it back and moved on. And yes, I put every bill back. Sure, the 50s and 20s would've filled my snack pouch nicely. (That's a joke, of course.)

Now the platoon has settled near the edge of the neighborhood, positioning ourselves to keep eyes on a busy intersection where insurgents have been placing IEDs. From the second floor of the house we've taken over, we can watch the spot all night, though it means we're here for the long haul. The family in the house is in for an inconvenient night, to say the least. While several Iraqis I've met seem grateful we're here, moments like this breed tension and frustration. This family isn't going anywhere until our job is done—they can't leave and risk tipping off neighbors about our position. It's another aspect of the job that gnaws at me, the way it disrupts lives, the unspoken tension that builds.

Second squad moves through, clearing the house as the rest of us wait in the courtyard with Sergeant Cromer and Doc. Across the way, 3rd and 4th squads and Lt. Chappell are securing the place next door. This house is surprisingly nice, even by Western standards. Ramadi is strange that way: one neighborhood might have shacks with dirt floors and tin roofs, while the next has villas with marble floors and AC. This place lands somewhere in between—comfortable, well-kept.

The man of the house offers us tea and pita bread, and I gratefully accept. It's hot, earthy, and the bread's fresh enough to remind me of home. I have a few minutes before my shift on the balcony, so I dig a treat out of my snack pouch, savoring it as I head outside. I leave my M4 inside, knowing we'll be using the SAW for overwatch.

Sergeant McInnis is in the living room, holding a radio to the homeowner's mouth while Lt. Chappell talks with him in Arabic from the next house over. I don't catch any of it, but I'm grateful for Lt. Chappell's skill—young platoon leaders catch a lot of flak for their lack of experience, but Chappell handles this job better than most. I wouldn't want the weight of 40 guys' lives on my shoulders, but he handles it well.

Out on the balcony, I settle into my hide, giving the SAW a final once-over to make sure it's good to go. Then I pull down my NVGs, night vision goggles, settling them over my eyes. I'm running PVS-7 Deltas, which cover both eyes. Some guys use the 14s, which are single monocle-style and allow you to keep one eye's natural night vision, but that always felt off to me. With the 7Ds, everything is one green-tinged world.

Half an hour drags by, and the strain starts hitting me—the NVGs are heavy, pulling down on my head and neck, and I'm running critically low on snacks. It's the type of shift that tests your focus. Staring through the green glow of night vision can lull you into a weird haze if you're not careful. But my relief shows up right on time, and I head back inside, glad to unbuckle my flak vest and helmet. The family let us borrow some pillows, which I gratefully accept, though I drape a spare t-shirt over mine—I've learned my lesson about hygiene. Last time, I ended up with ringworm from a communal pillow.

The night passes without incident, and we're still not moving out. Command wants us holding here a few more hours, watching that road, so anytime one of us has to go outside, we throw on a robe and headscarf to blend in, avoiding attention. It's a bizarre look, but if it works, I'm not complaining.

Hours crawl by with nothing to report—no movement, no contact. Finally, dawn starts breaking over Ramadi, casting a soft light over a neighborhood that barely noticed we were here. Another quiet night, but that's one kind of silence we can live with.

It's been over 30 hours since we started this mission, and finally, the call comes through: *endex*. Nothing sounds sweeter than hearing our platoon leader or company commander say those words. It means we're finally headed back to base. We're a mile out, moving back on foot in a staggered column, and exhaustion weighs on me—hours of grinding through neighborhoods, streets, and houses, pushing forward under a relentless sun and a sleepless night outside the wire.

I'm somewhere in the middle of the platoon, First Sergeant Adams beside me with one of his guys from headquarters. Up ahead, troops have already rounded the corner, the base about a half-mile away. I start daydreaming of fresh clothes and pulling off this sweat-soaked, dirt-caked uniform. But before the thought even settles, the ground shakes as an explosion rips through the street ahead, filling the sky with smoke, dirt, and debris.

It's a roadside bomb—a massive one. The plume of smoke and dust chokes the street, and I'm hit with a mix of shock and disbelief. An IED, right in the middle of our patrol on foot. The lead men had just taken a right, moving single-file. Their squad leader had called out to Sergeant Archie to cross the road, and he'd just set foot on the other side when everything went dark.

Archie doesn't even hear the blast; it's instant, his whole world swallowed in black smoke and debris. When he comes to, he's lying on his back beside Mullins, our forward observer, who's still clutching his M4. The radio crackles with panicked chatter as Sergeant Cromer's voice breaks through, calling for help.

"Get the fucking trucks! Archie's dead!" he shouts into his headset, his voice strained.

Archie blinks through the haze, hearing Cromer but barely processing. *I'm dead? I don't feel dead.* He sits up, and his voice cuts through the ringing in his ears. "Where the fuck are my guys?" he yells. "Yellow, Z, are you up?"

Mullins lies nearby, dazed, the ringing in his ears drowning out everything else. Bowden's voice reaches him faintly, calling his name, and Mullins stumbles toward him, still disoriented. He hesitates, his eyes on a nearby sand pile, wary of a second IED.

"You good?!" Bowden yells, running his hands over Mullins in a quick blood sweep. Thankfully, there's no blood—he's uninjured, at least physically.

Through the smoke, Sergeant Archie spots Hicks, who's rushing over with his usual wide grin, almost laughing, as if he's glad just to see Archie alive.

"I thought you just died!" Hicks exclaims, half-relieved, half-bewildered.

Archie, still propped against a wall, shakes his head, dizzy. "Me too, man. Me too. Are my guys up?"

Hicks nods, "Yeah, they're all up."

Fifty yards back, I'm staring at the smoke, a sick feeling settling in my stomach. The soldier next to me tells First Sergeant Adams he's going up to help with the bodies, and I feel dread wash over me as I jog forward, half-expecting to see blood and pieces of my friends scattered. But out of the haze, I see YellowHammer, one of the guys closest to the blast, running toward us, face smeared with soot, eyes blinking against the dust, but completely unharmed. Not one scratch.

It's nothing short of a miracle. I mutter a quick thanks to God and try to pull myself together. Sergeant Dubose is up ahead, shouting as he aims his rifle at a shack barely ten yards from the crater left by the IED. He hears movement inside, and I run up to help. We clear the building, finding only women and children. No men. Dubose and I exchange a look—the kind of look you give when you realize someone had set that bomb right next to where these people were staying. Dubose just shakes his head and shrugs. Behind us, Sergeant Cromer is rallying the squad leaders, trying to pull the platoon together fast.

"We need to move, now!" he shouts. "When you're up, let me know!"

Lieutenant Chappell's voice crackles through the headset, steady and insistent. "Let's double-time it the fuck out of here."

Squad leaders sound off as Cromer checks in with each one.

"First Squad?"

"Up!"

"Second Squad?"

"Up!"

"Third Squad?"

"Up!"

"Fourth Squad?"

"Up!"

"Then let's move the fuck out!"

The air is thick with smoke, dust swirling in the dim morning light—a literal fog of war. But we press forward, moving as one, an intact platoon. The exhaustion I felt before is gone, adrenaline pumping through me as we jog through alleys and streets, weaving our way back to Combat Outpost. My legs are numb from hours of marching, but now, as I push through the Ramadi Mile, it barely registers.

We stop briefly at the railroad tracks just south of the base to regroup, each squad pulling 360-degree security. Even this close to the wire, we're cautious, but our break is seconds. As Chappell walks past YellowHammer, he notices the tear streaks on his face.

"Archie," he says quietly, "YellowHammer looks like he's crying. Check on him when we're back."

"Roger that, LT."

We slip through the front gate without further incident, and a few of us make a beeline for what we call the chow hall to see if there's anything to eat. No luck. This "chow hall" is just a half-ruined building with a few tables. The roof was blasted off by a mortar hit ages ago, and it's bare now. With no contractors out here, we're lucky if the cooks can scrape together a hot meal or two in a day.

Out at the smoke pit, Archie lights up a cigarette, passing one to YellowHammer.

"You good, man? You alright?" he asks, the concern clear in his voice.

YellowHammer takes a shaky drag, still pale, his voice low. "They almost got us, sergeant. They almost got us."

Chapter 8

The Cost of Courage
November 25th, 2004

Ramadi, a place where even the night feels hostile, like it's holding its breath. It's only November, and we've been ambushed and lit up nearly every time we leave the wire. Too many close calls, and I wonder if we've already bled our luck dry. My platoon's young, yet we're steady, keeping it together through gunfire, RPGs, and sniper shots. But what haunts me most isn't the rifles or the bombers; it's the IEDs – invisible threats lying in wait, patient as the desert itself. They're out there, under roads, inside walls. The thought of one ripping us apart keeps me praying harder than I ever have.

The sun's just gone down, and we're gearing up for a two-day mission. All on foot, moving out the north gate of Combat Outpost and threading our way west into the heart of the city. The mission tonight is a cordon and search, not a full-blown raid. This isn't about busting doors down, terrorizing, or using sheer violence to shake out the enemy – no, a cordon and search is a quieter beast. We'll knock instead of kick, keep the muzzles lowered, but don't mistake that for weakness. Nobody refuses us entry, and each home gets a thorough sweep. Most nights, we're just looking for military-aged men. If a gunpowder test on their hands or face comes back positive, we cuff them, haul them back to base. If it's negative, we move on, like ghosts through the neighborhood.

Right now, we're outside, assembling in the last few minutes before we head out.

"Squad leaders, get your men ready to go," Sergeant Cromer calls out, his voice low but urgent.

With Sergeant Dubose out on leave, Archie's taken over as squad leader. We're a bit short with Cassell out too on leave, but Archie's solid – sharp as hell. He checks each of us, making sure we're loaded up, carrying night vision, water, ammo, and a few MREs. He stops in front of me, scrutinizing my gear.

"You good, Stoke? Got all your shit?" he asks.

"Yeah, man. You?" I grin, just to keep it light.

"Yes, princess, I'm good," he laughs, giving me a nudge.

Out here, the usual military barriers are fading. Day after day, after the firefights and near misses, our squad's become something different – bonded through survival, more brothers than anything else. Nobody really minds.

Sergeant Cromer's voice cuts through again, quiet but foreboding. "Hope you all are right with God," he says, to no one in particular.

A chill runs through me. Before I can dwell on it, the LT's voice crackles over the radio.

"Alright, let's move out," Lieutenant Chappell orders.

We're just a few paces out when we hear it – a *thunk*, then a soft, high-pitched *whistle* in the distance. Every man in this platoon knows exactly what that sound means.

"Incoming!" someone shouts.

In an instant, we scatter. Some of us bolt back inside, others dive behind the nearest Humvee.

BOOM!

"Fuck! Our chow hall!" someone shouts.

Not the chow hall, I think, feeling a stab of irritation. The chow here's already dismal, and now we're down a roof too. The hit makes me feel oddly personal, like the enemy just took a swipe at my last shreds of comfort. Another mortar slams into the ground outside the base. We brace, anticipating a third – they usually come in threes. But this time, silence follows. No third round. Weird.

I can hear the mortar teams behind us scrambling in their pits, sending rounds back in response. How they get such a quick fix on the enemy's position is a mystery to me; it's like black magic. All I know is that within seconds of incoming fire, they're dropping rounds right back, letting whoever's out there know we're not here to take it lying down. Out of the corner of my eye, I see Archie scanning the area.

"Anybody hit?" he calls out, a bit breathless.

Everyone's unscathed, and my soul's the only thing taking a hit as I watch smoke rise from what used to be our chow hall roof.

Lt. Chappell's voice is back on the radio, sounding impatient. "Let's go! SP time is now!"

We regroup, stepping out the back gate and falling into formation through the cemetery in a staggered column. Night's closed in around us, and our night vision goggles cast everything in eerie shades of green. Depth perception's shot, but we've learned to navigate like this, to make it work. We've barely made it a few hundred meters when the order comes through to halt and hold position.

I frown, whispering to Moret, "I know we're not near the AO yet – what's the holdup?"

He shrugs, grinning, and calls out to Archie. "Sergeant Archie, what's going on?"

"Schuh has to take a shit," Archie mutters.

It's both absurdly funny and painfully unfortunate; the entire platoon is now on high alert, maintaining 360-degree security just so he can take a dump. And as much as we'd like to laugh it off, the poor guy's battling dysentery, on antibiotics, and has no control over it.

The rest of the patrol to our AO is uneventful. When we arrive, we find an abandoned schoolhouse to use as a base, securing it quickly before setting up for the night. Some of the guys settle in to catch a few minutes of rest while others pull security on the rooftop. At dawn, Sergeant Archie learns he'll be picking up extra responsibility: three combat engineers will be attached to us, and he'll be in charge of them on top of his squad leader duties.

My turn for an overwatch shift comes up, so I grab a snack from my assault pack and head up to the roof. Down below, Archie and first squad are getting acquainted with the engineers, who'll help us sweep for IEDs. They're trained for it, though in practice, they're often doubling up, doing infantry work just like us.

Forty-five minutes pass in the quiet, broken only by distant gunshots. Perfect time for a snack. Digging into my pouch, I pull out the "dessert" from my MRE—a piece of lemon pound cake. It's nothing fancy, but it hits the spot. I wash it down from my Camelbak, wishing I had a cold Dr. Pepper instead. Can't always go to war with the snacks you want; you go with the snacks you've got. Isn't that the saying?

Beneath me in the schoolhouse, Sergeant Cromer, Lt. Chappell, Mullins, and Doc Meyer are shooting the breeze, talking about everything from home to women. Mullins pulls the main course out of his MRE heater, about to dig in, when a single sharp *crack* interrupts. Instantly, everyone drops into combat mode, the casual chatter replaced with grim focus.

I scan my sector but don't see anything. Then the sound hits me—agonized cries, coming from a rooftop a few buildings over. Private Grant from another platoon has been hit, a sniper round straight to the chest, somehow missing his body armor.

Inside the schoolhouse, Sergeant Archie jumps to his feet, grabbing Doc Meyer and his aid bag. The LT and Mullins follow close as they head toward the building where Grant was hit. On the way out, Cromer grabs Mullins by the shoulder.

"If you aren't on the LT's ass, I'm gonna fuck you up!" Cromer growls, a fierce reminder.

Poor Mullins can't catch a break—his orders bounce between Lt. Chappell, who sometimes tells him to "wait here," and Sergeant Cromer, who's always barking at him to stay glued to the LT. Mullins half-jokes that it's like "mom and dad fighting over me."

They reach the base of the building where Grant's down. The only access to the roof is a ladder on the outside, no staircase in sight. Once up top, another soldier frantically asks Archie to help locate the sniper. Archie just stares at him.

"I don't have a scope, dude. What do you want me do?"

"Just help us look; we think it came from over there," the soldier points to a nearby building.

Archie takes a quick scan, spotting a figure on a distant rooftop looking in their direction. A team heads over to investigate, only to find it's just some guy hanging his laundry. Meanwhile, Mullins notices another man watching intently from an adjacent roof.

"Sir, I've got a guy here who keeps looking our way," Mullins reports.

"Then keep a fucking gun on him, Mullins!" the LT snaps.

Up on the roof, Grant is struggling for breath, writhing in pain. Doc Meyer wastes no time. He removes Grant's flak vest, cuts open his blouse, and examines him, concluding it's likely a tension pneumothorax—air is trapped in his chest cavity, collapsing his lung. Doc reaches for his needle to perform a chest decompression, a risky but necessary move.

The LT looks over, visibly uneasy. "You sure you know what you're doing?"

If anyone knows what they're doing, it's Doc Meyer, who spends every spare moment buried in a medical manual. He's almost certainly a better medic than the rest of us are infantrymen .

"Shut up and let him do his fucking job, LT," Archie cuts in, giving Doc space.

Focused, Doc finds the correct spot and carefully inserts the needle into Grant's chest. Archie's face lights up with recognition, and he nods.

"Dude! The fucking movie!" Archie says, grinning.

Doc looks up, catching the reference. "Yup."

They're talking about *Three Kings*, when George Clooney's character performs the same procedure on Mark Wahlberg. It's a decent depiction of what Doc's trying to do here: relieve the pressure to save Grant's life.

Doc does his best to stabilize Grant, and with Archie, the LT, and members of Grant's team, they carefully lower him off the roof. Grant's pained cries echo as he's loaded into a Humvee and CASEVACed back to base. Despite Doc's efforts, Grant will die from his wounds—a sniper took him out just a few rooftops away, close enough that I could've hit it with a thrown rock. The weight of that realization doesn't fully sink in until days later.

As Grant is evacuated, a new mission drops for us: a house search a few blocks away. When I come down from the roof, Sergeant Cromer is on the headset, trying to find Archie.

"Let's go, we're stepping out. Two-one, where are you?"

"I'm at the CASEVAC site."

"Well, get your squad—we're moving."

When Archie catches up to Sergeant Cromer, there's more weight waiting to be piled onto his shoulders.

"Archie, you got two Air Force guys and a couple of reporters tagging along," Cromer says, barely glancing at him. "And pick a house for overwatch – send Bravo team up."

The orders come fast, mid-stride, like we're gearing up for a drill instead of diving headfirst into enemy territory. Archie now has Alpha and Bravo teams, the engineers, the reporters, and the Air Force crew all under his charge. Meanwhile, he's expected to find an overwatch position, check the map, and assign my team to clear a house, all while keeping tabs on our objective.

"Cromer, what the fuck. This is too much." Archie's voice is taut, brimming with frustration.

"You got this, Arch."

Archie scowls but holds his tongue, spinning to us. "Hicks!" he says, jabbing his finger at a spot on the map. "Take your team and clear this house. Set up an overwatch while we go hit the target."

"Stoke, Patterson, Thompson, gear up – we got a house to clear," Sergeant Hicks tells us, his voice sharpening our focus.

My team moves with purpose. We sweep the house quickly, finding it empty, just another hollow structure in this shell of a city. The dust hangs thick, undisturbed except for our boots. Up on the roof, we take our corners, scanning every angle. It's second nature by now, but Hicks runs through it anyway, making sure every field of fire is covered. Experience has taught us you never trust a private to cover his own sector; too many things can be missed. From our vantage point, we see two blocks away as the rest of 3rd Platoon approaches the target house, the walls marked with bullet holes from battles past. It's a grim reminder that this isn't the first firefight this house has seen, and it won't be the last.

Third squad is moving in. As Johnson steps into the courtyard, he pauses, thinking he spots someone down the street—a figure motioning, almost waving as if to warn him off. But the moment passes, and he refocuses on the house.

Outside, Sergeant Archie and YellowHammer replace Schuh and Mutchler on security beside a three-story building. They're holding the left side of a T-intersection, their M240 machine gun aimed at a four-way intersection two blocks ahead, the same spot where Johnson saw that fleeting wave. As Schuh and Mutchler move to join third squad clearing the house, Archie is busy ensuring everyone is set, checking on the engineers and the Air Force guys, trying to account for every variable.

"Yo Bradley, you know what you're doing, right?" Archie asks, a tight edge in his voice.

"Yeah, man, we're good. We've done this before," Bradley, one of the engineers, says, nodding confidently.

"Then keep an eye on the windows and the rooftops. Anything moves, you call it out."

"Roger that."

Just as Archie finishes giving the orders, a woman in a faded hijab and a young girl walk past, slowing as they pass, the woman's eyes lingering on him with a look somewhere between disdain and fear. She keeps moving but, two blocks down, she glances back and starts talking to a man in a yellow jacket. He listens, nodding, then leads her aside. Archie's stomach sinks. *Oh shit.*
He turns sharply, voice low but urgent.

"Heads up! Watch the roofs and windows!" he hisses to Moret and YellowHammer, guiding them to better cover.

"Cromer!" he calls, trying to get through. "Shit's about to hit the fan."

Cromer barely looks back. "There's nothing going on, Arch," he mutters dismissively, underestimating the threat.

Ignoring him, Archie continues positioning the engineers, telling them to cover the corner two blocks ahead. But Cromer strides into the open street, disregarding Archie's instincts. YellowHammer starts to lower his guard too. Moret shifts, almost skeptical.

Then the man in the yellow jacket reappears, stepping out from the corner. For a brief second, there's a pause, like the air itself freezes – and then the world shatters. He raises a PKM machine gun, braced at his hip, and unleashes hell.

The air fills with a deafening barrage as bullets slam into the wall beside Archie and YellowHammer, the concrete erupting into clouds of dust and debris. Everything is chaos. The PKM's rounds are brutal, tearing through bodies before they even have a chance to hit the dirt. Archie dives, grabbing YellowHammer, but it's too late for some. Screams cut through the gunfire. The roar of that belt-fed monster echoes off the buildings, drowning out any orders, any calls for help.

In mere seconds, the ambush has taken a toll. We have multiple men down, the ground smeared with blood as soldiers scramble for cover, the few able bodies left pulling others out of the line of fire. It's a slaughter, and we're caught dead center.

YellowHammer's scream rips through the air as bullets slam into his feet and ankles, tearing flesh and shattering bone.

"I'm fucking hit!" he cries, his voice raw with pain as rounds chew up the dirt around him.

Archie swings his M203 up to return fire, but before he can pull the trigger, bullets find his weapon, shredding it before four rounds slam into his chest plate, knocking the wind out of him. He barely has time to regain his footing when two rounds tear into his left hand, spinning him sideways. As he stumbles, another volley hits his back, most rounds striking his rear body armor but jarring him with every impact.

Around him, the engineers are caught in the crossfire. Sergeant Bradley and Private First Class Bell are both hit repeatedly, bullets tearing through their legs and abdomens. Pijue is face-down, shrieking for a medic as blood pools beneath his shredded legs. In a matter of seconds, Archie and all three engineers are struck at least fifteen times, with rounds puncturing armor, ripping through flesh, and smashing weapons.

Inside the target house, third squad and Doc Meyer hear the relentless gunfire, punctuated by desperate calls for a medic. Doc doesn't hesitate. He bolts from cover and sprints into the chaos.

"Doc! Wait for the fucking fire to die down!" Sergeant Munger shouts after him.

But Doc doesn't look back, doesn't pause. He's already out in the open, charging toward the wounded. Bullets kick up dirt around him, snapping through the air, and then one tears into his leg. He stumbles, crashing back into the courtyard, pain searing through his body. But he hears Pijue's screams – the agonized, pleading cry for help – and he grits his teeth, pushing himself back up. Nothing matters now but reaching those men.

"Medic!" Pijue yells, his voice breaking with panic.

"Shut the fuck up and let the fire die down, Pijue!" Archie yells, while trying to throw himself over Pijue's body, in an attempt to shield him from further injury with his own battered frame.

Sergeant Archie, easily the smallest soldier in the platoon, is fearless. His slight, 135-pound frame hides the heart of a warrior, a man who has already survived a landmine in a previous deployment and wears the scars of it. As he tries to shield Pijue, another barrage finds him. One round skims off his helmet, another slams into his hip, and a third strikes him between his legs. He rolls off Pijue, locking eyes with the man in the yellow jacket – the one wielding the PKM machine gun. Archie tries to lift his weapon, but his hip is shattered; he can't feel his right side.

A few yards away, Doc Meyer assesses his own wound: a deep, ragged hole punched through his lower leg. He can barely tell what he's looking at – fragments of bone, torn muscle, maybe ligament. But none of it matters. He ignores the throbbing pain, forcing himself upright as more cries for help reach him, muffled by the relentless thunder of machine gun fire. With grim determination, Doc limps out into the open again, running straight into the hailstorm of 7.62mm rounds, his mind already cataloging what he needs to do to save them: hemorrhage control, tourniquets, airways. He mentally ticks off each step, preparing to treat every wound, determining his supplies even as he drags himself forward.

But before he can reach the soldiers, a bullet slams into his chest, punching through his body and out his lower left abdomen. The force of the impact throws him to the ground, leaving him sprawled just meters from the wounded.

Inside the house, the rest of third squad, including LT Chappell and Mullins, hear the hell outside but can't identify the source. The LT rushes out, leaving Mullins scrambling to keep up. Mullins races past Johnson and Lineweber, who are reporting to Staff Sergeant Munger.

"Get the fuck out there and start doing buddy aid!" Munger orders.

Without hesitation, Johnson and Lineweber sprint into the open toward the cries for a medic. Johnson, Sergeant Nace, and Sergeant McInnis reach Doc Meyer and start pulling him out of the line of fire. Doc's face is ghostly pale, his eyes glazed, but McInnis begins CPR, fighting to bring him back.

With every chest compression, a mix of blood and fluids spills from Doc's wounds, pooling beneath them. Kneeling beside McInnis, Johnson's hands and uniform turn crimson, soaking up the life draining from Doc's body. Sergeant Nace watches somberly as Sergeant McInnis works tirelessly, desperation fueling each push, each breath – until Sergeant Cromer steps forward, placing a hand on his shoulder.

"He's gone, Mac. You can stop."

Mac's shoulders slump, his face etched with disbelief. He looks at Cromer, almost pleading, but knows he's right. Private First Class Harrison J. Meyer, our beloved Doc, the one who would charge through gunfire to save his friends, is gone. He turned twenty just two weeks ago.

In the courtyard, Mullins spots Sweeney, panic evident on his face.

"Sweeney, where the fuck did the LT go?!"

Sweeney points toward the firefight outside. Both men know they have to act, and though fear gnaws at them, they share a grim resolve.

"Fuck it, let's go!" Sweeney says, the battle cry that's kept us moving all deployment.

They rush into the street, greeted by a scene of blood and chaos. Following a trail of crimson, they enter a courtyard turned casualty collection point (CCP), where the wounded are being dragged in from the line of fire. Johnson, Lineweber, Sweeney, and Mullins do their best to administer buddy aid, frantically working to save lives amidst the carnage. Up on a nearby rooftop, a squad leader calls out, desperately seeking IV fluids.

"Who has fluids? We need more fluids!"

"I've got a bag!" Schuh replies, digging through his assault pack before handing it over. "Who's hit?" he asks, barely processing the question.

"Everyone!" the squad leader yells, turning to sprint back to the CCP.

"We need a CASEVAC, ASAP!" LT Chappell's voice crackles over the battalion radio. "We've got multiple casualties!"

Overwhelmed by the chaos, leadership struggles to account for everyone.

"Archie, where the fuck are you?" Cromer demands through his headset.

"I'm fucking shot and can't move!" Archie's voice crackles back, strained and barely audible.

Seeing Archie and Pijue immobilized in the street, LT Chappell and Lineweber rush to them. The LT grabs Archie by the handle on his flak vest, dragging him into the CCP, while Lineweber hauls Pijue out of harm's way. Archie, barely conscious, notices an engineer slumped nearby, motionless. Pulling out a packet of QuikClot he got from Doc Meyer, Archie instructs a fellow soldier on how to apply it to the engineer's wounds.

"You're the bravest man I've ever met," Lineweber says, awe in his voice.

"Shut the fuck up and give him the QuikClot," Archie snaps, forcing himself to focus.

Archie is loaded onto the CASEVAC truck, and as the pain meds begin to dull his senses, he glimpses Sergeant Cromer standing nearby, their eyes meeting for the first time since the firefight began.

"I fucking told you," Archie mouths silently, pain and defiance mingling in his gaze.

"I'm sorry," Cromer mouths back, unable to meet his eyes for long.

As they prepare to move out, Sergeant Cromer and Johnson lift Doc Meyer's lifeless body, covered in a poncho. Johnson is struck by how heavy Doc feels, a weight that goes beyond his physical body.

"Why does he seem so heavy?" he whispers.

"It's dead weight, Johnson," Cromer replies, his voice flat and hollow.

Nearby, Mullins, unaware that Doc has died, loads gear into the humvee beside Doc's body, giving him a light pat on the leg.

"Hey man, you're gonna be alright!" he says, his voice thick with misplaced optimism.

From my position on the rooftop two blocks away, I listen in horror as my platoon is consumed by one of the bloodiest, deadliest skirmishes of our entire deployment. The machine gun fire is relentless, and I can't tell if it's our M240s or the enemy's PKM. Every sharp crack of an AK-47 jolts me, but the machine guns are harder to distinguish. I scan my sector, feeling utterly powerless, guilt gnawing at me for being in relative safety. I've never felt so helpless.

Minutes later, Sergeant Hicks approaches, his face grim. Patterson and Thompson join me to hear the news, bracing themselves.

"Well, Stoke...we're what's left of first squad. And Doc Meyer didn't make it."

"What do you mean he didn't make it?" I ask, numb.

"He's KIA."

"But he's our medic...he's supposed to be untouchable," I whisper, struggling to process it.

"They all got shot, Stoke. All of them. Even the engineers...just cut down."

For once, I'm at a loss for words. Numbness takes over, the shock mirrored in Patterson and Thompson's faces as we stare at each other in silence. Eventually, Hicks tells us to get back to our sectors, but nothing feels real anymore.

Thompson, who took an EMT course back in South Korea before we deployed, steps up to take over as a makeshift medic for the remainder of the mission. He's not Doc Meyer, but he's better equipped than any of the rest of us to patch up wounds until we can get a real medic back at Combat Outpost.

We hunker down in the schoolhouse for the night, each of us taking turns on rooftop security. The weight of the day hangs over us all, thick and suffocating, while the rest of the platoon tries to get a few hours of sleep. We still have an entire day of missions ahead, so some rest is crucial. But the air inside the schoolhouse is heavy with grief, anger, and exhaustion. Most of us try to bury what happened, shoving emotions into some hidden corner of our minds to be dealt with later – or maybe not at all. The mission comes first. Some handle it differently. Schuh sits against the wall, eyes red-rimmed as he quietly takes a drag from his cigarette, lost in thought. The rumor is that Doc will receive a medal, but none of us know the full story yet.

The next morning

I awake to the sound of a loudspeaker chanting the obligatory morning Islamic prayer. I have no idea what the clergyman is saying but I suspect he does not wish us, foreigners, well. At times, the ritualist prayer almost seems angry, these are the days to be extra vigilant, like this morning.

The events of yesterday haven't even begun to sink in. All I can do is pray that today's less violent, though part of me wants it to be hell – anything to let off this anger simmering inside. I crashed on the bare cement of this shitty, abandoned schoolhouse, barely catching three or four hours, but somehow, I'm not even tired. No one is. Every face around me is wired, grim with that lethal mix of exhaustion and fury. We're caught between two extremes: itching to kill some motherfuckers as payback for Doc and praying to get through the day without a single engagement. The knot in my gut twists even tighter as the imam's harsh, angry voice echoes over the rooftops, calling out morning prayer. It sounds like he's as sick of us as we are of him, and to be honest, it's unsettling as hell.

We gear up and move out, forming a staggered column down a dusty stretch of street. The neighborhood we're headed to looks a bit better kept than most of Ramadi, though it's far from anything you'd call nice. Here and there, newer bullet scars mar the walls. The air smells of stale smoke and ash, the kind that clings to you long after you leave. First and second squads spread out, cordoning off part of the area as we start the mind-numbing cycle of house clearing.

After the first few houses, autopilot takes over. You go room by room, sweep by sweep, each house a clone of the last. Autopilot's dangerous – it deadens your edge, makes you forget that behind every corner could be a rifle waiting to take you down. But it's easy to drift after house four or five.

I'm finishing up on the second floor of another house when I run into Sergeant Cromer on the stairs. He's talking to the owner through our interpreter, and I give him a quick nod that means "it's clear." Cromer returns the nod, shifting his attention back to the man.

Then, without warning, the familiar chaos erupts outside. The sharp crack of an AK-47 cuts through the air, followed by the snapping cracks of M4s and the steady thump of a light machine gun.

"Get to the roof, Stoke!" Sergeant Cromer yells.

I bolt up the stairs, my heart hammering as I reach the rooftop and scan for targets, praying for a clean shot. But all I hear are the screams – that raw, awful sound a soldier makes when they've been torn open by a bullet. I recognize the voice before I even see him: Thompson, my fireteam brother and our backup medic, has been hit. He's the one who was on the rooftop yesterday when Doc was killed, the one who volunteered to take Doc's place. Now, he's lying there, his leg shattered by a bullet that ripped through both his tibia and fibula. The pain must be unimaginable, and it kills me to know he's allergic to the pain meds carried by the CASEVAC crew. The poor bastard will have to endure it all, raw and unfiltered, until they can get him to proper medical care.

"Dammit!" I mutter as Thompson's CASEVAC finally hauls him away. I look at what's left of my squad and can barely process it. Normally, we're nine men strong; now we're down to a few exhausted souls barely holding together a fireteam. Sergeant Dubose and Cassell are on leave, Archie's shot to hell, YellowHammer's down, and Thompson's on his way back with a shattered leg. "What the hell happened to my squad?" I wonder bitterly, the reality settling in with a hollow ache. For a moment, all I want to do is light up anyone who dares look in our direction.

After Thompson's CASEVAC, we press on, pushing through the neighborhood for hours. By the time the commander calls endex, the tension in the air is as thick as dust. My patience with the locals is gone, replaced by a numb, frustrated anger. At first, we were knocking politely, showing some basic respect. But after Thompson got hit, it's a different story – we're banging on doors, ordering people out of the way, barely holding back the rage simmering beneath the surface. I know most of these people are just caught in the middle, but at this moment, it's hard to care.

Our platoon's taken such a beating that the brigade QRF – not just our battalion's but the brigade's – is rolling in to help us limp back to Combat Outpost. Now, instead of just humvees, there are battle tanks and Bradley Fighting Vehicles parked on nearly every street corner, keeping insurgents pinned down so we can make it out without any more casualties. I can only imagine what those tank crews think of us as we stagger past them, bruised, battered, heads held high but bodies wrecked. Every step sends pain radiating through my muscles, but all I want is to reach the outpost, strip off this gear, and collapse. A shower would be a miracle, but we don't even have that. And our chow hall – with its new hole in the roof – isn't much comfort either.

It's only November, and we have over seven months left. At this rate, I honestly don't know how we're going to keep going. But all we can do is keep moving, one brutal day after another. This is the grind, the reality of modern infantry – gritty, relentless, and unforgiving.

Chapter 9
The Other Side of War
November 26th, 2004
Worthington, Ohio

Over 6,300 miles away from the dust and danger of Ramadi, Iraq, a dark sedan pulls up to a modest suburban home in Worthington, Ohio. Two Army officers step out, their uniforms as crisp and perfect as if they were part of the very fabric of duty itself. They share a look—a silent, shared understanding of what they're about to do. The duty of delivering the news of a fallen soldier is one they're trained for, yet no amount of training can brace them for the gut-wrenching pain they'll bring into this household.

They make their way up the driveway with slow, purposeful steps, their polished shoes crunching softly against the gravel. For a brief moment, they hesitate before knocking, each man gathering his resolve, knowing the task never gets easier.

Inside, Kelley Meyer, the family's youngest, opens the door with a bright expression that fades the moment she sees the uniforms. Her gaze darts between the two men as fear settles into her chest, her instincts recognizing the solemn weight these soldiers carry.

"What's going on?" she asks, her voice small, her hands gripping the doorframe.

One of the officers, with a voice softened from years of performing this duty, replies, "We need to speak with Mr. and Mrs. Meyer."

"They're not here," Kelley says, faltering. "It's their anniversary. They're out for dinner."

The two men exchange a glance, digesting the bitter irony. They ask for her father's cell phone number, explaining they cannot share any information with her directly. As they dial the number, Kelley remains in the doorway, fear twisting her stomach. She senses that whatever she's about to overhear will change her life forever.

The phone rings as Bill Meyer, in a quiet booth at an upscale restaurant, reaches for his phone. A call from the Army mid-dinner makes his heart stutter. He listens as the man on the other end confirms his identity, asking him to verify his social security number—a procedure that feels absurdly bureaucratic in a moment fraught with dread.

Finally, the soldier on the line speaks: "Mr. Meyer, we regret to inform you that your son, Harrison, was killed in action today. We are incredibly sorry."

Bill feels a wave of nausea as the words settle in. His world compresses; all he hears is the harsh, hollow ringing in his ears. He squeezes his eyes shut, a single tear escaping, and clutches the phone tightly as though he might anchor himself to some semblance of reality. A hundred thoughts rush through his mind: his son's laugh, his dreams, the pride he had watching him grow. And now this—a parent's worst nightmare, unfolding over a phone call in the middle of an anniversary dinner.

Across the table, his wife Deborah watches as Bill's face transforms, shifting from confusion to a pain so deep that she reaches across the table instinctively. Her own heart pounds as she senses something irreparable has happened. As Bill's hand falls back to his lap, he meets her eyes, his voice barely a whisper.

"Debbie," he says, his voice breaking, "our boy was killed today."

A shocked silence blankets them as Deborah, in one agonizing moment, feels the foundation of her world shatter.

The car ride home is a blur, a journey marked by broken sobs and unspoken pain. Bill grips the steering wheel, trying to control his trembling hands as his wife beside him weeps openly, calling out their son's name as if he might still answer. In the passenger seat, Deborah holds her arms around herself tightly, keening with grief as her mind flashes through memories of Harrison: his first steps, his beaming smile, his stories from Iraq.

Bill knows he must remain composed; he has calls to make to family, each one more painful than the last. He dreads the call to Bronwyn, Harrison's older sister, who would protect him fiercely in life and now will have to live without him. When he finally dials her number, he barely manages to keep his voice steady.

The phone rings on Bronwyn's end, and she answers with a lighthearted, "Hey, what's up?" completely unaware of the darkness about to descend. Debbie, fighting back her tears, somehow musters the strength to say it plainly, knowing any hint of emotion will break her entirely.

"Bronwyn," she says softly, "there's something I need to tell you. Your brother was killed today."

Bronwyn goes silent, her mind struggling to process the words. She feels herself sink to the floor as her mother's voice continues, "Go to your front door. Your uncle and grandfather are waiting for you."

Moving in a daze, she stumbles to the door and sees them—two strong men from her family, standing helpless and tearful, waiting to catch her as her world collapses. Reality crashes into her, and she gasps for air, struggling to breathe through the suffocating weight of grief. She sinks to her knees, sobbing and retching, while her family holds her, trying to support her through this unimaginable pain.

The week drags on painfully as they await Harrison's body. The family barely eats, speaks, or sleeps; their lives are consumed by the profound sorrow that now fills every corner of their home. When Harrison's flag-draped coffin finally arrives at Dover Air Force Base, they stand in the November cold, shivering, numb to the chill but not to the heartbreak. Each family member holds a silent vigil, clutching onto their memories of him, steeling themselves for the days ahead.

The funeral is an overwhelming outpouring of respect and grief. Friends, family, and comrades gather to remember Harrison's life, a life of bravery and kindness that ended too soon. The strains of "Amazing Grace" played on bagpipes echo through the church, the sound piercing Bronwyn's heart. She grips her mother's hand as they listen, the music both a balm and a wound. Every time she hears it in the future, she'll feel her throat tighten, and tears will prick her eyes, a painful reminder of a song that is as beautiful as it is mournful.

In the days following the funeral, Bronwyn drifts in a fog of grief, unable to comprehend a world without her brother. She chain-smokes, numb to everything but the crushing pain, and begins to drink heavily, searching for an escape at the bottom of each glass. School feels empty and pointless, yet she drags herself through her exams. The weight of loss changes her, forging a fierce determination to live a life worthy of the brother she loved.

Thirteen months later, she makes the decision that will alter her course forever. She cuts ties with the Army Reserves and re-enlists for active duty, choosing to become a medic in honor of her brother. She excels in her training, graduating at the top of her class, driven by the memory of Harrison's selflessness. She serves another tour in Iraq, channeling her grief into service, dedicating her life to saving others, knowing that Harrison would be proud.

Back home, she buys a bright green Mustang, the car Harrison had dreamed of buying upon his return. Every time she drives it, she feels a connection to him, a symbol of the dreams he shared and the journey he started for her. It's her tribute, a way to carry him with her, to remember that even in loss, there is something of him that will live on in her.

Years later, Bronwyn is a skilled pediatric nurse practitioner, caring for critically ill children with compassion and strength. She knows that her journey has been shaped by Harrison's life and legacy. She is grateful for the person he helped her become, carrying his memory with reverence, knowing that few are ever so fortunate as to be loved by a soul as courageous and true as his.

Chapter 10
Close Calls and Cigarettes
December 9th, 2004

It's been over a week since Doc Meyer went down, and it feels like we've been running missions without a single breath in between. The loss hangs heavy, but the pace won't allow us a moment to process it. A Chinook lifted off this morning, dust in its wake and bodies strapped inside—soldiers hit by a sniper on patrol. One didn't make it out. The mission tempo just chews us up and spits us back out, as if we're cogs in some relentless, grinding machine.

I'm helping Patterson shove YellowHammer's things into a black plastic container. When someone goes down, his gear has to be boxed up, tagged, and sent back home, as if we could pack his whole life into a plastic shell. The truth is, out here, grief barely has a moment to settle. My only reliable feelings anymore are hunger and fatigue.

I toss the lid on the crate just as Sergeant Hicks strolls over.

"Op Order in 10 minutes," he says, and there's no sense of urgency in his voice, as if this is just another day in the desert. And maybe, for him, it is.

Patterson sighs, shaking his head. "Didn't we just get back from a mission an hour ago?"

"Nine out of ten days outside the wire," I mutter, snapping the lid shut on the crate. "Hell, I don't even know what day it is."

Ten minutes later, we're out in the dust, waiting for Hicks to brief us. I'm perched on an MRE box, popping Skittles from a stash I've been saving, each piece of candy a small rebellion against the monotony. Hicks keeps the briefing short.

"Same drill—secure the intersection, search a few houses, don't get shot at," he says flatly.

"Operation get shot at, got it," Patterson grumbles beside me.

He's half-joking, but we both know how these missions go. Hicks isn't a bad leader, but he's cryptic, barely giving us enough to guess what we're in for. Sometimes I wonder if he's leaving details out intentionally or if he just doesn't have them.

We finish boxing up Yellow's things and head to the trucks. There's something oddly comforting about the humvees—these heavy, rumbling beasts that are part mobile fortress, part rolling deathtrap. I refill my water, watching Cassell throw his gear into the driver's seat of Cromer's truck. I ask him how things have changed since he's been back.

"It's a total pile of shit," he says, flicking ash off his cigarette. "Everyone's got a 'fuck warning shots' attitude now, especially after Doc." His words are tight, like they're squeezing through clenched teeth.

"Yeah, no argument there."

Cassell's got this ritual of lighting up right before every mission. He smokes like he's charging up for battle, even though he's been chewed out for it before. There was that time he lit one up in the middle of a firefight, just ducked into a courtyard, shielding the lighter from the wind with his hand. It's like he's got his own set of rules for when and where smoking is allowed.

Another thing about Cassell—he was the Picasso of pin-ups, with a knack for turning our plain, dingy walls into a masterpiece of "interior design" that soldiers from other platoons would come by to admire. Every time he got his hands on an *FHM* or *Maxim*, he'd meticulously cut out the photos of the hottest models, and soon enough, the wall above our bunks was plastered with glossy faces and curves. What I thought was just a one-time project turned into a full-blown obsession. Every few weeks, Cassell added another layer of "decor," until every last blank spot was covered. By the end, the walls were a chaotic, collage of smirking red lips and sultry eyes, the whole room alive with a kind of racy, slightly surreal energy. It was like Cassell had single-handedly transformed our bare-bones quarters into a Playboy mansion fever dream, and honestly, it was hard not to be impressed.

The LT gives the signal to move, and we roll out, the convoy kicking up clouds of dust that settle on everything, coating our gear, our faces. Route Michigan stretches out in front of us, a long artery of cracked asphalt, flanked by rubble and an endless stream of graffiti-covered walls. When we reach Easy Street, we cross the median, and I feel my stomach clench. It's a spot we've crossed too many times, the kind of place that gives you the creeping feeling you're one lucky pass away from an IED.

We veer left, taking an alternate route because of a blocked road up ahead. The streets are noisy—chatter, children darting in and out of doorways, and the occasional motorbike sputtering by. Quiet streets mean trouble. Patterson glances out the window, muttering about how the blocked road could mean anything, but whatever it is, we're in it now.

"Alright Stoke, pull over here and face the humvee south. And watch out for that nasty ass pile of whatever the fuck that is," Dubose tells me, eyeing a particularly rancid-looking heap in the gutter.

The street here is nothing but rubble and refuse, sewage flowing down the curbs like an open, toxic river.

"Moret, make sure you get a good angle toward that intersection about 100 meters out," Dubose adds, and I hear Moret's reply from the turret.

Depending on the mission, sometimes a driver stays back with the gunner while the rest of the squad fans out. Today, I'm holding down the fort with Moret, and the rest of the team is out there in the heat, combing through houses, each one a potential trap. I lean against the door, glancing up at Moret.

"Watched *The Prince and Me* last night on QRF," I say, trying to distract myself from the tension twisting in my gut.

Moret laughs, eyes still trained on his sector. "Shoot man, Julia Stiles is a damn fine woman. I'd watch her in anything."

Moret had a distinctive way of saying "shoot" that never failed to catch attention. He stretched it out with a drawn-out "shooooot," the middle held long and deep, with a heavy emphasis on the "ooo" that dropped in pitch before tapering off. It was the kind of word that hung in the air, unmistakably his.

Across the street, Cassell and Schuh are covering an alley, keeping watch as they exchange their own banter. Cassell is peering down his ACOG, eyes trained on the end of the road. His body tenses as he spots something—a figure, just for a split second, a head popping out from behind a corner.

"Hey, Schuh, did you see that?" Cassell hisses, eyes narrowing.

"See what?"

"End of the road, on the right side. Some guy peeking around the corner."

Cassell shifts his rifle, finger hovering near the trigger. He's wondering if he should have taken the shot, but he hesitates, his breath catching. Schuh is saying something, but Cassell barely registers it. His vision blurs as he stares down the scope, and suddenly, the glowing red chevron in his ACOG seems to spin. Then he realizes it—too late.

"RPG!" Cassell yells, voice cracking with adrenaline.

Schuh doesn't hesitate; he opens fire with the 240, the deafening rattle of gunfire filling the street, echoing off the walls. Cassell dives for cover, instinctively going for the truck, but he pivots last second, thinking, *They're aiming for the truck.* He hits the ground hard, scraping his palms as he scrambles for cover.

Then it hits—a huge crack, the sound tearing through the air like lightning, but there's no explosion. Just a dull, solid *thud.*

"What the fuck just happened?" Cassell yells, heart hammering in his chest.

Schuh looks over, face pale. "An RPG just bounced off the windshield!"

Cassell stares, trying to process. "You're serious?"

"Yeah, it's sitting right there," Schuh says, pointing.

The two of them watch, wide-eyed, as Sergeant Cromer sprints over, his face a mask of confusion and disbelief.

"What the hell happened to my truck?" he asks, voice tight with shock.

"RPG to the windshield," Cassell says, barely believing his own words. "Didn't go off."

Cromer glances down at the RPG lying at his feet, picking it up by the tail. "Idiots forgot to pull the pin," he mutters, turning it over in his hands like some bizarre trophy.

The LT radios in, ending the mission, and we pack it in, the truck rumbling back to base. On the way, Schuh leans over, hand shaking slightly as he pulls a cigarette from Cassell's pack. The last time I saw him smoke was over a week ago; he'd just quit, determined to kick the habit.

"Gimme one, Cassell," he says, barely getting the words out before the cigarette is between his lips.

Schuh smokes the whole pack on the way back, barely taking a breath between drags, the smoke curling up from his lips in a steady stream. Two weeks later, he's back out here, and this time, another RPG hits his humvee, exploding on impact. Miraculously, he makes it out unscathed, the cigarette dangling from his lips as if it's the only thing holding him together.

After that, he doesn't even pretend he'll quit. "There's no damn way I'm kicking this habit out here," he says, taking a long, steady drag, the smoke drifting into the hot, heavy air around us.

Chapter 11

Tension and Turrets

Mid-December

I can't remember the day. Tuesday? Wednesday? I don't know if it's morning or afternoon; my watch is still on the makeshift stand by my bed. We've been outside the wire for hours now, running another cordon-and-knock. Humvees got us partway, but I'm a dismount. That means walking, lots of walking.

Sweeney and I are paired up, clearing houses. He used to run the radio for Lieutenant Chappell for a while when Mullins wasn't doing it until YellowHammer got hit. Now, he's our second SAW gunner, and he's alright by me. Bit of a nerd—watches anime non-stop—but he knows his way around a SAW and has my back. That's what matters.

Next house up, and this gate is giving me hell. I yank, but it barely moves. There's a car jammed on the other side, but if I can get it to budge, we're in.

"What's the holdup?" Sergeant Dubose asks, his voice laced with impatience.

"Gate's stuck," I grunt.

"Kick the motherfucker open."

I wind up, throw a hard kick into it, but no dice. Rusty as hell, but still holding strong.

"Sweeney, you're up." I'm more than happy to let the other guy handle it.

Sweeney, taller and a little bit heavier, takes a few steps back, and instead of a kick, he body-checks it like he's hitting a linebacker. The gate collapses off its hinges, smacking the ground inside the courtyard and nearly taking out the car's bumper. Sweeney stumbles, trips over the fallen gate, and lands half-sprawled across the car's hood.

"Holy shit, Sweeney!" Dubose exclaims, half in shock, half in laughter.

But what gets us is the homeowner. He's been sitting in the car the whole time, and none of us even noticed. Awkwardly, he gets out and faces Sweeney, who stammers,

"Uh... sorry, dude."

The guy's not happy, but he lets us into his place anyway. We search, find nothing, and I'm left wondering how many more locals we're pushing toward the "get out of our country" side.

In the distance, we hear the familiar "thunk" of mortars leaving the tube, scattered gunfire in the background. Not a day goes by without some firefight, if not ours, then the Marines to the west.

"Did that sound like mortars to you, Stoke?" Dubose asks.

"Yeah, definitely not an RPG. Too much of a low thunk."

"Not our problem today," Dubose mutters, more hopeful than certain.

Dubose and I, we both want to kill bad guys, but we'd rather not break a sweat doing it. Just as we're hoping for a quiet day, a call comes in. Mortars are firing from within our AO, which means it's our problem now. The LT has orders to hunt down whoever's launching them, so he splits us up to cover more ground.

We're operating in the southeast section of Ramadi today. There's a stadium in the middle of it, where Sweeney once caused a fiasco ramming through a locked gate with the humvee. That time, he managed to shear off the M240's carrying handle and sights on the concrete arch above. It's a story none of us will ever let him live down.

The LT sends Sergeant Dubose, Sweeney, and me a block south while he and his humvee stay north of us. We're moving west on foot, staying in sight of the LT's humvee for overwatch. Three blocks in, gunfire erupts to the south by the stadium. Dubose halts us and fiddles with the radio, but nothing's coming through. He tries calling the LT, and again, silence. He even checks in with the platoon channel, but it's dead.

We keep moving, hoping to pick up comms when we hit Easy Street and link back up. The gunfire to the south is getting louder, and I go to high ready, finger hovering over the selector switch.

Several blocks ahead, a humvee blazes across the intersection, heading south on Easy Street.

"Uh, Sergeant Dubose, wasn't that the LT's humvee?"

"Yup, sure was, Stoke. That motherfucker," he mutters, frustration boiling.

Dubose has a decision to make—either chase the LT or regroup with the platoon. But with no trucks nearby, it's just the three of us, standing in the open with zero comms.

"Stoke, Sweeney, let's go," Dubose says, adjusting his rifle. "We're doing the Ramadi mile, boys."

Fantastic. Running with all our gear—my least favorite part of the job. I choke down some water from my Camelbak, and off we go toward Easy Street.

Running patrol in the open is a nerve-wracking dance. One guy covers an intersection while the others run past, then repeat at the next street. We move like this until we hit Easy Street and head south, each stop bringing fresh sweat and gritted teeth.

We finally see the LT's humvee turning east back toward the stadium. Dubose is pissed enough to be funny if the situation weren't so damn risky. We speed up, double-timing it through empty streets, storefronts closing as we pass. Closer to the stadium, the gunfire is louder, more sporadic, and the streets have emptied.

Two blocks out, three masked men in black sprint down a side street. We're too far to be certain they're armed, but instinct takes over. We unload in their direction as we cross the street, probably not hitting anything but sending a message. Almost certainly insurgents, likely the same guys firing on our men up ahead.

We reach the stadium and comms crackle back to life. Dubose spots the LT and storms over.

"You left us out there flapping in the wind, LT!" he snaps.

"First platoon was taking fire, and you're here now, aren't you?" the LT shrugs.

The trucks are parked, holding down an intersection near a line of houses we're about to search. I'm crammed into the back seat, drained from the mad dash down Easy Street earlier. My legs ache, heart still pounding from the adrenaline dump, and my stomach's growling for anything edible. Combat hunger is a thing no one warns you about, and I'd kill for a handful of stale M&Ms.

The streets around us are surprisingly busy. Vendors haggle, locals stroll, and kids dart between stalls, laughing. Busy streets are a good sign—places like this empty out fast at the first hint of trouble. Behind me, Bapst, Saffell, and Sikonia are spread out in the other truck, keeping watch. Bapst is behind the wheel, Sikonia's in the backseat, and Saffell's up in the turret, scanning the street with the .50 cal. They're bantering, trying to keep things light, but Bapst's tone shifts when he notices something a little... off.

About half a block away, a man steps out of an alley and freezes. He's staring right at us, eyes fixed on our trucks. Bapst tenses, watching him closely. "Heads up, guys," he mutters, loud enough to get Saffell's and Sikonia's attention. The man isn't doing anything outright threatening, but something feels wrong. He keeps glancing over, then disappears into a shop, only to reappear, stopping again to size us up. After a few minutes of this back-and-forth, he finally retreats into the shadows of the alley. Bapst watches him go, the hairs on his neck standing on end.

A hush creeps over the street. Vendors pull down tarps, doors slam shut, and in minutes, the once-busy market has turned into a ghost town. A sick feeling settles over us as every shop down the block closes, one by one.

"Yo, Saffell," Sikonia growls, a tremor in his voice. "Watch the fuck out, man. I don't like this."

Saffell, up in the turret, watches the emptying street with laser focus, his hands gripping the .50 cal. He's preparing himself for what he knows is coming. It's the silence before the storm, that terrible moment when you're just waiting for the first shot to crack the air. Less than a minute after Sikonia's warning, it happens.

The man from earlier bursts from the alley, this time holding an RPK machine gun. He charges straight into the middle of the intersection and, before any of us can react, drops to the ground and sets up. The gun goes prone, bipod down, aimed right at us, directly into Bapst's line of sight. Without a second's hesitation, he opens fire, the RPK's staccato ripping through the air.

"DOWN!" Bapst yells, ducking behind the steering wheel as bullets pound into the windshield.

The laminated glass splinters under the barrage, holding, but just barely. Saffell, up top, curses as the .50 jams almost immediately, locking up just as the first bullets from his end leave the barrel. He's up there fighting with the beast, trying to clear it, hands moving frantically while rounds chew into the front of the humvee, peppering the splash shield and sending shards of glass and metal scattering around him.

In the backseat, Sikonia's had enough. He's sick of waiting, feeling like a sitting duck.

"Fuck it!" he roars, kicking open the back door and leaping out with his SAW, using the humvee door as makeshift cover.

He drops to one knee and fires, emptying a hundred rounds into the man's direction. The street fills with the smoke of burning powder, each flash from Sikonia's SAW adding to the chaos.

Pinned down under Sikonia's spray of fire, the guy in the intersection loses his nerve. He scrambles backward, dragging his RPK and disappearing behind cover. Sikonia doesn't let up, blasting every inch of the alley where the shooter had been. He's pretty sure he hit the guy, maybe even dropped him, but we'll never know. A getaway car is almost certainly waiting, ready to whisk him away just as fast as he appeared. It's happened before: an ambush, a hasty retreat, and the shooter gone by the time we reach their hiding spot.

Sikonia fires off a few more rounds, breathing hard, then ducks back into the humvee, slamming the door behind him. The gunfire stops. Silence returns to the street, dust settling over the empty market. Bapst stays low for a beat, waiting for another attack, but nothing comes. The tension hangs in the air, thick and charged, as we wait.

Finally, Saffell manages to clear the .50, slapping the receiver closed and readying it again. He's panting, his eyes wild from the close call, but there's no one left to shoot. The street remains empty, lifeless. We exchange glances, mentally assessing each other, but no one's hurt. The truck took most of the damage, the windshield a cracked mosaic of splintered glass and pocked metal.

After what feels like a long, tense minute, the LT's voice crackles over the radio, checking in. "Everyone good?"

"Yeah," Bapst answers, a bit shaky, "all good here." He pauses, then with a bitter laugh adds, "But damn, I could use a new windshield."

They laugh, a dark, gritty kind of laughter that only combat can produce. The relief doesn't last long, though. We still have houses to clear, streets to secure, and a long day ahead. It takes a few more hours of patrolling, but the day winds down without another engagement. No injuries, no more gunfights, and not a sign of the guys who fired mortars at us earlier.

Another mission in the books, another day survived. But deep down, a familiar frustration simmers. It's always the same: hit-and-run attacks, ghost-like shooters slipping away before we can pin them down. It's enough to drive you mad if you let it. For now, though, we let the hum of the trucks soothe the nerves. We're back on the road, and for tonight at least, we get to live another day.

Chapter 12

Explosive Cargo
December 27th, 2004

My platoon is on QRF today, the Quick Reaction Force. We're staged with our Humvees right at the front gate, vehicles packed out for whatever mission may drop, waiting for the go. This also means we're crammed into the QRF room—sleeping bags, gear, and snack packs all piled up—so if a mission drops, nobody's scrambling to find anyone. The walls are coated with that distinct smell of body armor and sweat, reminders of yesterday's mission.

QRF can be called for anything, but nine times out of ten, we're either backup for a squad in deep trouble or hauling a wounded soldier back to the Combat Outpost. Sometimes, QRF is just dead quiet, and we pass the time playing cards, watching worn-out DVDs, or throwing jabs at each other over last night's chow. Today? Today's not that kind of day.

"Get to the trucks, men! We're moving out!" Sergeant Cromer's shout cuts through the chatter.

I swig down the last of my water and toss a couple of MRE desserts into my snack pouch—small luxuries for long hauls. You'd think after enough of these runs, I'd be packing extra ammo first, but the snack pouch saves you in ways bullets can't on these marathons.

"Stoke! Get the truck fired up," Sergeant Dubose barks as I jump into action.

"What's the gig this time, Sarge?"

"Intel just came in on a high-value target. We're headed out for a raid," he says, shrugging like it's nothing new.

"Sounds thrilling."

"Don't get too pumped. We're the drivers—another squad gets the real fun."

We load up and roll out through the front gate, engines roaring as we head into Ramadi's winding streets. Raid missions are different. Guys' pulses pick up, fingers inch closer to the triggers, and the anticipation's almost a tangible thing in the air. Five minutes in, we turn onto the road leading to the target house. I spot our informant, face covered and tense, riding shotgun in one of the gun trucks. His job's simple: point to the house and get out of sight. My truck's midway in the convoy, and I pull off two houses down, facing left. My gunner and I get out, eyes scanning the shadows, and lock down our section of the road.

A raid can go from zero to a hundred in a split second. If insurgents are inside and ready, they'll light us up the moment the door flies open. Our infantry doesn't have the high-tech stuff, just rifles and the occasional flashbang if we're lucky. Flashbangs are like temporary blindness and chaos in a can, but they're hard to come by. We're not special forces—just line infantry.

I glance back as the breach man kicks in the door, the rest of the fireteam pouring in behind him. For these close-quarters gigs, they swap the heavy SAW gunner for an M4 guy—no one wants to clear rooms with a machine gun. No gunfire—good sign. We stay sharp, watching every angle, until it's time to roll.

Within minutes, the door opens, and out come three of our guys hauling computer towers and CDs spilling from their arms. The sight is almost too good.

"Guess nobody was home," I say to my gunner, chuckling at the chaos.

"Looks like we just raided a Radio Shack," he mutters, grinning.

"Stoke! Pack it up, we're moving!" Dubose shouts, signaling it's time to get back in line.

Fastest mission of the battalion, hands down. Less than 20 minutes out the gate, house hit, computers nabbed, and we're already inbound to Corregidor. This kind of quick-action mission is my speed. Sitting around drives me stir-crazy, so these rapid-fire raids keep me sane. Once back, the intel we grabbed goes to the S2 shop—the intel guys. They comb through the files, CDs, whatever we dragged in, while we settle in for whatever downtime QRF can offer until the next call comes.

It's been hours since we wrecked that dude's place, and night has swallowed up Corregidor. I'm deep into an episode of *Smallville*, half ignoring the world, thinking of what I'll say to Dubose when we break down the latest plot twist. But then, I hear Lieutenant Chappell's voice cutting through: he's calling for squad leaders. Probably means Baker Company's in the shit and needs us outside the wire.

"Get your shit, we're heading out again!" Sergeant Cromer yells.

I slam my DVD player shut and reach for my flak vest. At some point, someone decided to call these things "plate carriers" and designed them less like medieval armor, but right now, it's just bulky gear that does the job. Twenty pounds of Kevlar, plus water and any extras, and I don't even feel it now. It's crazy how that becomes part of you out here. Before deployment, the weight made my neck ache—now, it feels like putting on a second skin.

"What's the mission?" I ask my team leader.

"Baker Company wants support. We'll find out the details on site," Hicks says.

"Roger that."

It's a dark, quiet ride out to Baker's AO. We roll up, and as we get closer, word starts filtering through. Baker's just raided a bomb maker's house and found a VBIED. Two trucks back, Private First Class Johnson's sitting in his humvee's backseat when he overhears the radio chatter. Then, third squad leader Staff Sergeant Munger, riding up front, confirms the crazy news: Baker needs someone to drive this damn thing back to Corregidor. Munger clicks his mic off, turns, and without a second's hesitation, eyes Johnson.

"Let's go, Johnson."

Johnson's face says it all, but he clambers out, grumbling as he and LT Chappell make their way toward the house.

"Sir, am I seriously about to drive a fucking car bomb back to base?" he asks.

"C'mon, Nasty J, it's not like you've never stolen a car before," LT says with a grin.

"Yeah, but not one wired to blow, sir!"

"You'll be fine, Johnson," LT says with a slap on the back.

As Johnson slides into the driver's seat, the weight of that decision to join the Army sits heavy. "What a stupid-ass decision that was," he thinks, half-joking, half-serious. The inside of this thing stinks like raw gasoline, and he can't miss the pile of wires snaking out of a pager and into the cigarette lighter. And the seat? Set for someone a foot shorter, and it doesn't adjust, so Johnson's knees are crammed up.

"Am I really driving this piece of shit?" he mutters, gripping the wheel. No turning back now.

As we roll out, every bump is a test of Johnson's nerves. The car's got some janky wiring, so every little hit sends the interior lights flashing, washing out his night vision goggles. The brakes are so sensitive, each tap smashes his NVGs into the windshield. The humvee behind him radios in, begging him to stop hitting the brakes since it's screwing with their NVGs too.

"This is so fucking bonkers," he mutters, hands white-knuckling the wheel. The guy's talking to himself, which, given the circumstances, isn't all that crazy.

We crawl our way back, and by the time we reach Corregidor, Johnson's nerves have stretched so far it's a miracle he can get out of that rig. Johnsons's balls have grown so much in the short ride back that he can barely step out of the vehicle when he tries but damn, he's earned every bit of respect we can give him.

Life at Camp Corregidor and Combat Outpost isn't just different from Camp Ramadi or TQ—it's another universe altogether. Those bigger camps have resources we can barely imagine: showers, porta-johns, real chow halls. Here? We've got none of that. The closest we get to a bath is when the rain floods the trenches, and as for restrooms, well, we've got tubes to piss in and buckets to shit in that get burned with diesel fuel every day. Maybe that's why half the platoon is down with a rotating case of the runs.

Our chow situation is about as glamorous as you'd expect. Our cooks really do the best that they can with what they have to work with, but, they just don't have anything to work with. Entertainment? That's whatever scratched-up DVD somebody left behind, passed from guy to guy until it's more static than picture. Rumor has it there's a makeshift gym somewhere, but until I see it with my own eyes, I'll call it a myth. Hell, who am I kidding, I wouldn't use that thing even if it were right next door.

One thing we do have in ample supply, though, is grit. Call it courage, call it resilience, but it's probably more accurate to say we've got balls of steel. And this isn't some casual claim. For Christmas, the brigade command staff decided to try bringing us some "holiday cheer" this year— they came rolling in from Camp Ramadi, dressed in Santa suits, their tank's barrel strung with Christmas lights. They came with hot chow and good intentions, sure, but about ten minutes in, the mortars started whistling.

They didn't stick around to help, though. The commander and his entourage bolted, barely taking time to pack up the chow line before they tore out of here, shells bursting behind them. For us, though, dodging mortar rounds is just another day. We've been shelled so often, half the guys don't even flinch anymore unless the blast is close enough to feel the heat. At least it feels like they bolted quick, it's quite possible they just had more chow to drop off but I'd like think we young grunts are just more battle hardened then everyone else.

Chapter 13

Oops, Didn't Mean to Interrupt. Oh, and nice robe dude.

January, 2005

Alright, new year, new me. Let's go out there and do some great things for Uncle Sam. Gonna be a good year. I just know it.

"Stoke, you're on shit-burning detail today," my team leader says without missing a beat.

"Roger that."

So, it's a bit of a slow start to the year, alright, but everyone's gotta start somewhere. For those not in the know, shit-burning detail is exactly what it sounds like—nothing more, nothing less—and, believe me, it's as revolting as it sounds. No port-a-johns here; we have makeshift stalls behind Dog Company's barracks. A toilet seat is the one tiny luxury we've scrounged, so at least we're not bare-assed on rough wood. But beneath each seat is a cut-down 55-gallon burn barrel filled with an impressive day's worth of, well, evidence that men eat nothing but MREs and chow hall sludge. Flies buzz around the piles like it's their personal buffet before they dart off to land on your face. No wonder everyone got sick last month. On the bright side, rumor has it we're getting a shower trailer soon. I've had three showers in the last two months. I'm disgusted with myself.

The process is simple: fill the barrels with diesel or JP8 and light them up. I'll stress this one detail because it is absolutely crucial: diesel only. JP8 if you must. Not regular gas under any circumstance. I learned that the hard way. I grabbed the wrong can once and lit that barrel like it was the Fourth of July. The flames shot up so fast I should have known something was off, but I figured, 'eh, it'll work itself out.' By the time I added more fuel, I was practically juggling flames. A fireball chased the stream of fuel right back up to the jerry can. I dropped it and bolted. By then, flames were spreading all over the burn area.

"Uh oh."

In a mild panic, I ran upstairs to wake Sergeant Dubose.

"Sergeant Dubose," I mutter, trying not to freak him out.

"What do you want, Stoke?"

"Uh, I started a fire out back."

"What? How bad?"

"I don't know, but I think the camp might burn down."

With a frustrated groan, he tells me to grab a fire extinguisher from the 998. Great advice—except when I got back, the damn thing was empty. After a mad dash to the "chow hall," the cook hands me a second extinguisher, and thankfully this one spews white foamy goodness all over the flaming disaster zone. The barrels are a little worse for wear, and the ground around them? Blackened like a marshmallow left in the campfire.

Later, I ask what went wrong, and they tell me I used gas instead of diesel. Nice, wish somebody would have told me that but it's only my second time on this nasty detail, so live and learn.

The month has barely started, and we've already lost several guys I knew well. One of the hardest to believe is Staff Sergeant Vitagliano, "Sergeant V," from Charlie Company—a man built like a living GI Joe. I'll never forget the way he drilled his squad back in Korea, making them polish their boots in the middle of the field like they were about to meet the general. And yet, in a moment, a VBIED took him and PFC Geer, though he somehow shielded one of his guys and saved him. It's chaos here, and I've stopped counting the number of memorials. Each service is the same. Amazing Grace on the bagpipes, and that final roll call when they call the fallen's name three times, waiting for the reply that will never come. It doesn't get any easier. They say we're only halfway through this tour, and I don't want to imagine what the next six months will bring.

January 21st, 2005
1600 hours

I'm getting anxious. Iraq's first election is tomorrow, and it's our job to keep the peace. The city is buzzing with threats against anyone brave enough to vote, but all we can say is, "Don't worry about it." Well, not me—I'm just here to pull security, not to give pep talks. Our schedule is brutal, a night patrol tonight followed by two mounted patrols tomorrow. My arms are already aching just thinking about it.
2230 hours

We're seven minutes into the patrol, and I'm over it. I'm carrying the SAW tonight, technically a light machine gun, though it doesn't feel light at all. Better than the M240 the gunners lug around, but I swear I'm going to start hitting the gym after this.

"Stoke, you look tired. Get any sleep?" Sergeant Dubose asks, somehow reading my mind even in the pitch dark.

"Nope, I'm good though. Could go for one of those Yellow Jackets Bronstad used to pop like Skittles."

"Yeah, me too, man. Me too."

As we get a final check from Sergeant Cromer, we load up election fliers and staplers, ready to plaster the town in public service announcements for the next few hours. We step out of the back gate, weaving our way south, hugging the canal until we hit Baseline. From there, we turn west, deeper into the city. Every so often, we pass a few locals sitting around a deck of cards, waving as we pass. Weirdly peaceful, considering we're decked out in gear that screams "war zone."

When we reach the AO, one guy starts stapling fliers on a corner. I wish we were posting something badass like concert ads—something like, *"Live at Combat Outpost! One Night Only! Metallica!!! Come get your face melted off!!!"* But no, it's probably something like, *"Get out and vote, hope you don't die."* I don't even know what these fliers say, but I guess it doesn't matter.

After a few hours of canvassing, we finally approach the target house. The whole squad knows the drill, and we're moving like we're on autopilot by this point, our bodies in sync with our training.

Sergeant Cromer gives the command, "First Squad, you're up," and the team falls into formation, moving quietly, weapons at the ready, watching each other's backs.

Dubose signals to Hicks to lead his team in. We're stacked up by the doorway, tense and ready. There's always this edge before entering—what's waiting on the other side is anyone's guess, and we all know the horror stories about doors being rigged or surprise booby traps. Sweeney's in the lead, clutching the SAW, his eyes narrowed behind his night vision as he eases the door open. I'm actually not entirely sure how and why the SAW gunner is in the lead but sometimes you just roll with whatever feels right at the time, and this time, Sweeney is in the lead.

And that's when it happens. Sweeney freezes. Just... stops dead, his SAW raised and aimed at what turns out to be the most unexpected sight we've encountered in all of Ramadi. There, in the dim light, is an old man and a younger woman caught mid-coitus (mid-sexytime), staring wide-eyed right back at us.

The entire scene hangs in suspended animation for a beat. The guy's eyes go wide, and with a squawk, he scrambles for something to cover himself. He reaches for what must be the only thing nearby—a neon-pink silk bathrobe—and yanks it on, his face going from shock to a glare of pure, silent fury. The girl beside him doesn't know what to do, so she just... giggles, nervous and embarrassed but laughing nonetheless.

Sweeney, meanwhile, is as frozen as the two of them, his SAW still pointed directly at the old guy's chest.

"Sweeney," Hicks mutters, elbowing him, "SAW down, man. They're not exactly armed."

Sweeney blinks, lowers the barrel, and clears his throat. We all shuffle in behind him, and even though the situation is ridiculous, we're still doing our job. Each room gets a quick sweep. Sergeant Dubose and Hicks take point on asking questions, but we all know the chances of them spilling any intel are slim to none after this little disruption.

I feel the old guy's eyes on us the entire time, burning holes through the back of my head as we look around. He's standing there, arms crossed, fuming in his hot-pink bathrobe, likely cursing every American and their dog. I don't blame him. I'd be pissed too if a bunch of soldiers kicked in my door, interrupted *that*, and then rifled through my stuff.

We finish up and regroup at the door. Dubose throws an apologetic look at the man and nods, a silent "sorry" that probably doesn't help. The guy grunts, the girl waves, and we file out, trying to hold it together until we're a few blocks away and out of earshot.

The second we're out of range, Sweeney mutters, "What the hell was that?" and Hicks snorts, muttering something about "cockblocking for freedom."

We're still laughing as we get back into formation, a rare bit of levity for a place like this. No weapons, no intel, just a couple caught in an awkward moment. I'd say we might've made a friend, but I doubt it.

The rest of the night goes by in a quiet haze of fliers and darkened streets. By the time we get the call to exfil, I'm ready to crash. It's nearly 0430 when we step back on base, and Dubose tells us to get some sleep. We've got 3.5 hours before we head out again.

4 hours later

I slept like crap, so today's bound to be a real gem. At least we're taking the trucks out this time. The plan? Standard neighborhood rounds. Show presence, maybe knock on a door or two, just to remind everyone we're here and won't be leaving anytime soon. If I'm lucky, I'll be able to zone out in the back of the humvee until we're ready to do something. But man, I'm so tired I can barely keep my eyes open as we roll through the front gate and turn left onto Route Michigan. I'm hoping this is a smooth mission, but in my gut, I know that's not in the cards.

I must've passed out for a minute or two because when I open my eyes, we're parked, and dudes are already dismounting. I blink, trying to shake off the fog.

"Yo, Moret, what's the plan?" I mumble, still groggy.

He gives me a look. "Pulling security. What else?"

"Got it."

I plop down on the street, prone with my SAW, aiming west toward an intersection. It's a quiet spot, which, apparently, is all my tired brain needs to slip into sleep mode.

"Yo, Stoke, open your eyes, man!" I hear Moret yell. I mumble something unintelligible, but nothing changes.

"Stoke! Wake the hell up!"

"I'm awake, man, chill."

A few minutes later, Moret's yelling again.

"Stoke! Pull security!"

"I'm listening for gunfire, man," I say, half-joking, half-sincere.

"You better keep those damn eyes open!"

That jolts me a little—getting caught napping on security would be a surefire way to catch hell. I settle in, doing my best to stay alert, and try to shake off that creeping exhaustion.

The day wore on with the kind of dull exhaustion that made the heat feel heavier, every bead of sweat a reminder that vigilance was as draining as the mission itself. We moved to another neighborhood, the cycle repeating like a somber ritual. I shifted to a kneeling position instead of prone, trying to fend off the drowsiness that threatened to pull me under. My SAW was ready, its weight digging into my arms as I kept it pointed down the street, watching for any movement.

Behind me and facing the opposite direction, Schuh manned the turret of his humvee with King positioned outside, pulling security with his M14. The sun glared down on us, throwing sharp shadows against the cracked walls of the buildings. Schuh's binoculars were up, eyes scanning every corner, every shadow. Suddenly, his posture stiffened.

"Yellow jersey, southeast intersection," he called out, voice low but laced with tension.

I couldn't see the guy from where I was, but the air shifted. The hum of distant conversation and the shuffle of feet died away as if the entire city was holding its breath. A cold sliver of awareness trickled down my spine

I shifted again, trying to catch a glimpse, but from my angle behind the humvee, all I could do was listen. The seconds dragged on. Schuh's eyes tracked the figure as he disappeared and reappeared, moving between corners and peeking out from behind walls. The man was too deliberate, too aware.

"Alright, I know this game," Schuh muttered. "He's scouting us."

And just like that, the streets emptied. The few people lingering outside vanished into buildings, shutters clapped shut, and a hush fell over the city. My grip on the SAW tightened, every sense on high alert.

Then the gunfire erupted, tearing apart the silence. The unmistakable rattle of a PKM machine gun reverberated through the streets, metal slamming into metal as bullets chewed into Schuh's humvee. The windshield cracked, a web of shattered glass that miraculously held. The thud of rounds striking the ground was deafening, and I could only listen as chaos played out on the other side of my position, my view blocked by the vehicle's bulk.

The deep, staccato roar of the M240 unleashed a relentless stream of fire, the bursts chewing through brick and stone, filling the air with dust and debris. I craned my neck, heart racing, catching the sounds of King shouting something unintelligible before the sharper crack of his M14 punctuated the roar of the machine gun.

"RPG! RPG!" King's voice, sharp and urgent, cut through the chaos.

The air seemed to pause for a fraction of a second before his shot rang out. Even from my angle, I felt the impact; the RPG gunner never got his chance. I don't know if it was Schuh or King but one of their bullets found the insurgent mid-step, and his body jolted, the launcher slipping from his grasp as he toppled face-first into the open sewer running alongside the street. The dark, filthy water splashed up, soaking the corpse in a mix of waste and grime. It was a grotesque end, his body half-submerged, the yellow of his jersey smeared and stained.

The PKM gunner, seeing his partner go down, faltered. Schuh's M240 ripped into the corner he tried to retreat behind, and for a moment, it seemed like time froze. The gunfire ceased, leaving only the echoes bouncing off the cracked walls and my pulse thundering in my ears.

"Clear! All clear!" Sergeant Cromer called out.

I exhaled, the tension coiled in my muscles starting to release, though my hands were still white-knuckled around the SAW's grip.

Schuh climbed out of the turret, sweat and dirt streaked across his face, eyes still narrowed with adrenaline. King approached the RPG gunner's lifeless body, giving it a quick look before muttering, "Face down in the shit. Fitting."

Schuh smirked, pulling the RPG up off the ground next to the dead Muj fighter. He slung it over his shoulder as if claiming a prize and met King's raised eyebrow with a shrug.

"It's going up in the room. Call it decor."

Back in the humvee, I could only imagine the sight: the RPG launcher, a trophy of defiance, hanging on the wall of Schuh's corner like a grim testament to our daily grind. Moret glanced back at me as the convoy started to roll, his expression half-relieved, half-exhausted.

"Stay awake this time, Stoke."

I shot him a smirk, still hearing the faint echo of gunfire in my head. "Trust me, I'm wide awake now."

It wasn't a huge victory, but it was something. A reminder that we were still here, still holding on, still fighting. And in this place, even that counted for something.

We regroup and load up, heading back to base. Moret gives me grief for dozing off, which, yeah, I probably deserve. But lugging this SAW with 900 rounds has me drained.

"Yo, Stoke, you know the combat load is only 600 rounds, right?"

"Wait, what?" I blink, not quite following.

"600 rounds, genius."

"You mean to tell me I could've dropped that extra ammo drum?"

Moret smirks. "Guess you should've asked."

With an exasperated groan, I unclip the extra drum, relieved to shed those ten pounds. We've got two hours until our next SP, so sleep's off the table. Instead, I decide to check if Moret's got any of those frozen pizzas stashed away. Pizza beats any MRE hands down—well, maybe with the exception of Chili Mac, but that's sacred.

The third patrol goes off without a hitch. Nothing noteworthy. I'm dead on my feet but grateful to be moving without that extra ammo weight. And tonight, I get a hot shower—our platoon's day with the new shower trailer. Once a week isn't much, but after two months of barely any showers, it's heaven.

Later that night, I join Sergeant Dubose to unwind. We throw on *Smallville*, and I thumb through a sci-fi book I found lying around, *Satellite City*. I haven't read anything for fun in... ever, but it's nice to escape, even if it's only for a few minutes.

January 31st

The elections were yesterday, and it went off surprisingly quiet, at least in our sector. We spent all day outside the wire, patrolling to keep the peace. I heard turnout across Iraq was decent, around 60%, but in our area, Anbar Province, it was probably closer to 2%. Can't blame the locals; they'd probably feel safer staying home.

The good news? I just found out Johnson and I scored a four-day pass to Qatar next week. A break couldn't have come at a better time.

Chapter 14

Four-day pass
February 8th, 2005

"Dude, I hear you can have a couple of beers a day while on pass at Qatar," Johnson says, his eyes squinting against the morning sun as if envisioning a future far removed from the heat and grit around us.

"Not my thing, man. Plus, I'm only 20," I reply, a hint of a smile playing at my lips. It feels strange, thinking about beer and relaxation when the echoes of Ramadi are still fresh in my mind.

"I'm willing to bet 20 is fine," he says, a stubborn spark in his eyes. Johnson always had this way of clinging to hope, even if it was made of sand and wishful thinking.

"We'll see. Let's just get there first," I say, throwing my assault pack into the back of the humvee.

The hollow space in the vehicle reminds me again that I'm unarmed, and that unfamiliar vulnerability settles over me like a shadow.

The drive to TQ is uneventful, marked by the low rumble of tires on packed dirt and the dry whir of the wind through the cracked windows. The horizon is a relentless line of ochre, broken only by distant silhouettes of watchtowers and the occasional convoy. Without a rifle, every bump on the road feels magnified, each glance out the window a small act of vigilance. But for a chance at even a few days of reprieve, I'd make this journey ten times over.

When we arrive at TQ, the base sprawls before us, a jigsaw puzzle of sand-colored tents, concrete structures, and endless space that stretches far beyond what feels necessary. It's quieter than Ramadi, but there's a busyness here that hums with routine rather than danger. Johnson and I share a look of mild relief—this is as close to normal as we get.

"Hey guys, looking for a ride or something?"

The voice pulls me from my thoughts, and I see one of the interpreters who's come with us on a few missions. His face, marked by a week's worth of stubble, looks relaxed compared to the strained faces we're used to.

"Yeah, chow hall and PX if we can swing it," Johnson replies. His voice holds a casual hope that I almost envy.

The interpreter nods, motioning us toward a pickup truck that looks like it's survived more than a few misadventures. The paint is sun-bleached, and the body rattles when we step in. Without ceremony, he reaches beneath the dashboard and hotwires the truck. Johnson and I exchange glances—a silent understanding that, here, the unusual is commonplace.

"People call me T-Rex," he says as the truck roars to life, a grin peeking through his rough beard. "I'm with the interrogation teams when I'm not out with you guys."

That explains a lot. We settle into the seats as T-Rex weaves through the base with an ease that suggests he's done this a thousand times. The air is thick with dust, coating everything in a fine layer that sticks to sweat and fabric alike. I watch the makeshift streets blur by, feeling the tension ease just a notch.

The chow hall is a relief, a bustling space filled with chatter, the clinking of silverware, and the faint scent of real food. The trays in our hands feel heavier than usual, loaded with warm meals that remind me of home in an abstract way. Johnson eats with the quiet urgency of someone who doesn't trust good things to last, while I take a moment to savor it—chewing slowly, letting the simple act of eating feel like a victory.

Afterward, we hit the PX, its shelves stocked with small luxuries that seem decadent out here: snacks, new DVDs, even fresh socks. I grab a few essentials and pause at the phone center. The tinny voice on the other end feels like a lifeline, and I close my eyes as I listen to my parents' updates, their concern disguised behind cheerful questions.

"I'm good," I say, forcing a lightness into my voice that I'm not sure I feel. "It's quiet right now." The lie is small, and I let it stand.

The following morning, we're back at the air terminal. The sun is already making its slow climb, heating the sand until it radiates beneath our boots. We wait, shifting on metal benches that scrape against concrete and listening to the monotonous drone of announcements. Hours stretch, punctuated by the occasional nod or muttered joke from Johnson to break the silence.

Finally, an officer approaches, his expression weary. "Your pass has been canceled," he says, the words heavy and final.

"Wait, what?" Johnson and I say almost in unison, disbelief making our voices sharper.

"Paperwork issue. Sorry, guys."

The apology is almost more frustrating, the sympathetic tone a reminder that this isn't anyone's fault we can name. Johnson clenches his jaw, eyes fixed on the officer's back as he walks away.

"This is messed up," he mutters, more to himself than me.

"Typical," I reply, a bitter chuckle escaping before I can stop it.

The letdown settles over us like a weighted blanket, familiar but no less suffocating. We spend the rest of the day wandering with T-Rex, who shrugs when we tell him what happened.

He drives us around as if to say, "At least you're not completely stuck."

We stock up on more snacks and movies, consolation prizes that feel small but necessary.

That evening, Sergeant Dubose is waiting when we step off the transport back at base. His eyes scan our faces, reading the disappointment that hangs heavy in the air.

"Stoke, we'll do everything we can to get you back on the list for leave, alright?" His voice is steady, a lifeline I'm too worn out to grab onto.

"Roger that, Sergeant," I reply, the words automatic.

Johnson stands beside me, arms crossed as he looks out at the familiar, dusty sprawl of Corregidor.

"Next time, we'll make it," he says, a note of defiance in his voice.

I nod, letting the sentiment echo inside me.

"Yeah. Next time."

The sun dips low on the horizon, casting long shadows across the base, and for a moment, we stand in silence, the weight of missed chances sinking into the ground beneath our boots.

Chapter 15

Drivers and Gunners

Sometime in February

The muted crunch of boots in dirt and the clinking of metal tools set the soundtrack as Patterson planted the back blade of his shovel deep into the pile of sand. With a practiced motion, he scooped a hefty load and poured it into the gaping mouth of the sandbag Sikonia held open, fingers tensed around its coarse edge.

"You're Colonel Gubler's gunner now, huh?" Sikonia asked, his voice laced with both curiosity and a touch of disbelief.

He twisted the mouth of the bag shut and set it aside, dusting sand from his palms.

"Yeah, man. Dubose is pissed." Patterson smirked, though his eyes, shaded by a layer of sweat, betrayed a mix of pride and frustration.

"How'd that come to pass?" Sikonia probed, picking up another empty bag.

"Well, the commander's first choice was one of the cooks. First time they got shot at, the guy froze like a deer in headlights. Didn't even return fire, just ducked down inside the turret."

"Hell, for real?" Sikonia's eyebrows shot up as he let out a whistle.

"Yup. After that, the Colonel said, 'No more non-combat guys,' and pulled me. Guess I was in the wrong place at the right time."

A chuckle bubbled up between them, punctuated by the metallic clink as Patterson shook off stray sand. The wind shifted, carrying with it the acrid tang of oil and smoke from the maintenance yard. I glanced over, squinting against the sun, to see Saffel laughing alongside an Iraqi Commando who was working next to him, muscles taut and gleaming with sweat.

"Saffel! Where'd you find your new best friend?" I called, half-amused, half-genuinely curious.
Saffel flashed a grin that could have lit up the dingy barracks.

"Paid him five bucks to fill sandbags for me," he replied, his voice laced with mischief.

"Five bucks? You're a damn genius," I admitted, shaking my head with a smile.

The Commando, shirtless and wearing a pair of dark, mirrored sunglasses, worked with a fervor that put the rest of us to shame. His pace was relentless, each filled bag tossed to the side with a practiced flick of his wrist.

The moment of light-hearted banter shattered as the distant *thunk* and the shrill whistle of incoming mortars sliced through the air.

"Incoming!"

The call ricocheted around the sandbag pit. Bodies scattered, muscle memory kicking in before thought. Most dove behind barriers or flattened themselves into the shallow trenches carved into the base's hard ground. Patterson and Sikonia, though, stood motionless, their eyes meeting in a resigned exchange.

"Dude, I don't care," Sikonia muttered, as if commenting on the heat.

Patterson's noncommittal shrug said more than words. The chorus of footsteps and urgent shouts blurred, replaced by the low rumble of an impact and the screech of metal as a mortar punched a hole through the hood of a Humvee. Dust and smoke curled up in lazy tendrils, but no alarms sounded—no screams indicated a hit. This was normal now. Too normal.

Even the urgency of danger waned as the months dragged on. We'd all become reckless, flirting with the line between vigilance and numbness. It was a survival tactic; caring too much dulled your edge. I wasn't sure which was worse—constant hyper-awareness or the creeping indifference that dulled everything like static.

A few days later, I found myself reassigned for just one day as a driver for another platoon.

Sergeant Dubose's voice, sharp and familiar, had cut through the morning haze: "Stoke, first platoon needs a driver. Get moving."

While I knew a few guys in first platoon, they weren't my family. Driving for a new platoon always carried an edge of unknown. Some guys flinched at the first crack of gunfire, others leaned into it. I stole a glance at my TC as we prepared to roll out. He fit the look of the archetype: dark sunglasses, jaw set in a way that told me he thrived on the thin line between order and chaos. Sometimes, appearances didn't lie.

I didn't know the plan beyond a vague assumption: another cordon and knock. That was the bread and butter of our operations. The streets outside the gate unfolded like a canvas of dust and cinderblock as we eased into the city. The hum of idling engines harmonized with the murmured radio chatter. Once in position, our dismounts leaped out, weapons at the ready, while the gunner and I stayed behind, watching our slice of the world.

Minutes trickled by. The weight in my bladder, a trivial discomfort, became insistent. I hated going in the open, even though the streets were often streaked with filth and sewage. But necessity overruled modesty. I sidled between the Humvee and its door, fingers fumbling at my belt. The relief was instantaneous, if only for a heartbeat.

The clatter of the MK19's (pronounced mark 19) firing burst from above me, louder than thunder, each round a hammer blow to the air. My pulse spiked. Instinct dropped me behind the door, rifle clutched to my chest, trousers half-buttoned. The gunner's shouts blurred with the roaring bursts. I took in the chaos: my boots now damp from my interrupted piss, the tang of sweat and urine sharp in my nose, the heat of panic and realization that this was the first time I'd heard the MK19 up close. My platoon does not utilize this weapon so I was unfamiliar with it and my god, is it a beast. It's an automatic, belt-fed, grenade launcher that is hell for the enemy.

By the time the gunner paused, the air was heavy with silence and the distant patter of running boots. An insurgent had set up a machine gun just yards away, cut down before he could fire. I exhaled, tension ebbing with the realization that I was still intact.

But moments like these left marks. As of the time of this writing, October of 2024, I still have an incredibly difficult time taking a piss in public places. Like, I have to sit down, close my eyes, and sometimes cover my ears just to relax enough to urinate. I have seen a urologist and nothing is physically wrong so I only surmise it has something to do with that MK19 ruining an insurgent's day while I was trying to relieve myself. Some strange form of PTSD or something. The mind plays tricks, and mine hasn't let go.

Chapter 16

In the Crosshairs

Late February

"Man, that building's about to crumble. I hope Second Squad stays safe," I mutter to Sergeant Dubose, my eyes glued to the jagged silhouette of a structure that looks ready to fold under its own weight.

"Yeah, it's seen better days, but they'll be fine, Stoke," Dubose replies, his voice steady and reassuring from the passenger seat, though his eyes tell a different story—keen, calculating, always one step ahead of the worst.

I scan the cityscape, a patchwork of bullet-ridden facades and pockmarked streets. This part of Ramadi is a breeding ground for trouble, the kind that eats away at your nerves and keeps you half-awake even when you should be dead tired. Second Squad, tasked with overwatch, is perched in the center of this chaos. Their job: keep eyes on an area crawling with insurgents while we prowl the streets below, hoping to draw out gunfire and reveal enemy positions.

I reach into the cooler, smaller than our old standby, Combat Betty (rest her soul), and hand him a soda. It's a small comfort in this place, alongside the occasional sweet tea Dubose brews that almost matches my dad's.

In the Hide

Second Squad moves through the remnants of their stronghold with practiced efficiency. The building's first floor is a jigsaw puzzle of broken concrete and twisted rebar, the aftermath of an artillery strike. They climb the precarious rubble to reach the second floor, laying claymore mines at the only viable entry point—a silent promise to anyone thinking of sneaking up on them.

"Dude, if an RPG hits this place in the right spot, we're all screwed," King mutters, sweat darkening the band of his helmet as he adjusts his grip on the M14 rifle.

"No shit. It's a death trap," Avery replies, extending the bipod of his SAW, its weight a familiar burden.

Mac, their sergeant, leans against a crumbling wall, scanning the street below with a gaze that could slice steel. His men rotate the M14 rifle, sharing the long, watchful shifts. The SAW gunners, with their relentless light machine guns, keep fingers twitching near the triggers.

First Light

The first hint of dawn seeps across the skyline, shifting the world from black-and-green NVG glow to shades of muted orange and gray. Eyelids flicker as night vision goggles are removed, necks cracking as helmets are adjusted. The tension releases, only for a second.

Sergeant Nace, whose eyes haven't left the street, stiffens.

"Car! Three Hajis getting out—and they're putting on masks!" His voice, though low, carries a sharp urgency that snaps everyone into action.

Below, three figures step out of an old, beaten car painted in the typical orange and white stripes that make every soldier's pulse quicken. The men wrap their heads in black cloth, obscuring faces now marked by purpose. One hugs the building corner, checking the street. The other two wrestle an RPG and a PKM machine gun from the back seat.

"Light 'em up," Mac's command is almost a whisper, but it cuts through the room like a gunshot.

King lines up a shot through the spider hole, every heartbeat a hammer in his chest. The moment he pulls the trigger, dust explodes into the room, choking his vision. He curses and fires again, this time into the blur. Avery's SAW thunders beside him, filling the air with the metallic taste of cordite. Dirt and stone chip away, raining down as they unleash a storm of lead.

"Cease fire!" Mac shouts, his voice rising over the chaos.

As the dust settles, the street outside reveals two motionless bodies sprawled in pools of dark crimson. A third figure, a smudge of movement, vanishes into the maze of narrow streets.

The Bradley Arrives

A low, rolling rumble vibrates through the building—the unmistakable approach of an M2 Bradley Fighting Vehicle. The 27-ton metal behemoth roars down the road, its 25 mm chain gun and M240 machine gun bristling with threat. The building trembles as it passes, mortar dust spilling from cracks in the ceiling. Mac's eyes widen as pieces of concrete shift.

"Everyone, get down!" he orders, and the squad instinctively hits the floor.

"Not here, you idiots! Get out!" Mac bellows, waving them toward the gaping back wall, exposed to the city's wrath.

Avery doesn't hesitate. "Fuck it! I'll go first!" he shouts, tightening the sling on his SAW and tossing his assault pack to the ground. The rebar twists under his boots as he climbs down, teeth clenched. When his boots hit dirt, relief floods his face. One by one, the squad follows, the fear of exposure replaced by the electric pulse of survival.

At the Trucks

"That gunfire was way too close!" my gunner shouts, eyes searching the horizon from his perch in the turret.

"3-6, 3-2, over," Mac's voice crackles through the radio.

"Go for 3-6," the LT responds, crisp and composed.

"Contact. Two enemy KIA, weapons-laden vehicle. Third insurgent fled," Mac reports.

"Roger that."

We spring into motion as soon as the first shots echoed, tires kicking up dust and gravel. McInnis's voice feeds updates into our ears as we roll toward Second Squad's position.

The fleeing insurgent is soon pinned to a warren of narrow alleys, the Humvees cordoning off the area. Soldiers dismount, boots hitting the ground like an orchestra of chaos. I stay by the humvee, eyes darting between my gunner and the motion around me, ready for anything.

A shape shifts behind a fruit stand—a glint of metal. My stomach drops as an RPG emerges. Before I can shout, a fireteam stacks against the house next to it. LT Chappell's voice slices through the noise, barking orders in Arabic. The occupants inside shuffle nervously, except one. His chest heaves, eyes wide and wild. The gunpowder test strip darkens almost immediately.

"Detain him," LT says, without pause.

The man's wrists are cinched behind his back, a black hood pulled over his head. He's led to the 998, where a guard stands watch, and just like that, he's a number in the endless tally of war.

Dubose's grin appears like a sudden storm as we survey the prize—the bullet-riddled car, its seats full of AK-47s and RPGs.

"Cassell, you up for a drive?" Dubose asks, his tone a mix of challenge and mischief.

"Depends, Sergeant. This isn't another car bomb, right?"

"Relax. Just a ride."

Cassell mutters under his breath as he takes the wheel, but the engine refuses to cooperate, gurgling once before dying. The car, punched full of holes, becomes a burden. Cassell climbs into the front seat, now little more than a prisoner as the vehicle is hitched to our humvee. Each lurch forward rattles him, every bump a potential death sentence on these bomb-riddled streets.

"Stay sharp, Cassell," Dubose calls, eyes scanning for any sign of trouble.

The convoy rolls out, Cassell gripping the wheel with white-knuckled intensity, every pothole a reminder of how easily metal and flesh can be torn apart. He's living a twisted version of demolition derby, the car behind him dragging its wounded body past shattered storefronts and burned-out shells of cars that never made it.

By the time we reach the tracks near Corregidor, the LT decides it's time to lighten the load. We offload the weapons into the 998, sweat dripping, hands moving faster than thoughts. Dubose drops a thermite grenade onto the car's engine block, flames searing metal as the vehicle goes up in a blaze. Another car down, another memory scorched into the streets of Ramadi. Six cars, maybe seven. Not a bad day's work.

Chapter 17

Hollywood Lied - The Suppressed Truth
Early March

The sun had slipped below the city skyline, leaving a dusky glow that faded into the deep blue of night. Camp Corregidor settled into its usual nighttime hum, punctuated by the low rumble of generators and the occasional shout from a nearby outpost. Beyond the wire, Ramadi stirred with its own rhythm—sporadic noises that hinted at a restless city.

From behind a patchwork of camouflage netting and sandbags stacked tightly like a poor man's masonry, PFC Cassell struck a match, lighting a cigarette. The brief flare cast a flicker of light on his face as he took a drag, letting the smoke roll into his lungs. He scanned the cityscape, sweeping over rooftops and alleys that seemed to whisper secrets. Cassell lowered his binoculars, smoke curling lazily from his lips, and raised the barrel of the M14, its suppressor gleaming under the moon's faint light. His mouth lifted in a slight grin.

"Dude, I wanna take a pop shot," he muttered, more to himself than to Cheney, who stood next to him, shifting his weight and watching Cassell with a mix of skepticism and amusement.

"Are you fucking serious?" Cheney's voice was sharp, eyes narrowing as he tried to gauge Cassell's expression.

But Cassell was already toying with the M14's bolt, fingers restless and eager.

"Yeah man, I'm serious."

The M14 had been a staple of the platoon since their deployment, a relic refitted with a new suppressor that begged to be tested. Cassell nor Cheney have ever shot a suppressed weapon before so this whole thing is new to them. Cheney looked out at the city, wondering what unlucky target Cassell had in mind. He licked his lips, dry from the desert wind and nerves.

"Do you think it will be quiet enough?"

Cassell's grin widened. "We're gonna be able to take all kinds of pop shots and not be heard," he said, giving the rifle a reassuring pat.

Cheney snorted. "Do you think it's as quiet as it is in the movies?"

"Sure, man. Why wouldn't it be? This thing is badass."

"What are you gonna aim at?"

Cassell scanned the horizon until his eyes settled on a dim light bulb hanging from the second floor of a building in the distance. It glowed weakly, defying the dark.

"How about that lightbulb over there, a few hundred yards at our one o'clock?" Cheney suggested.

"Deal."

Cassell ground his cigarette into the sand and shouldered the M14, its weight familiar and reassuring. The scope centered on the lightbulb, which seemed unaware of its fate. He took a breath, exhaled slowly, and squeezed the trigger. The shot cracked like a whip, breaking the silence and pounding their eardrums. For a moment, everything was noise and shock, their ears ringing as if an invisible hand had slapped them.

"Dude, that was so fucking loud!" Cheney shouted, eyes wide.

The radio crackled with urgency.

"This is SOG, what's the situation?" The voice was sharp, cutting through their stunned silence.

Cassell's eyes darted to Cheney. "Dude, what the fuck do we tell him?" he hissed, panic tightening in his chest.

"Towers! Sitrep!?!" The sergeant's voice barked again, more insistent.

They sat frozen until another tower finally broke the silence.

"This is Tower 3, heard something but didn't see any movement, over."

"Roger, everyone stay alert," the SOG said, irritation in his tone.

Cassell exhaled, adrenaline coursing through him as he quickly pulled off the suppressor and stuffed the parts into his backpack. The weight of what they'd just done settled heavily between them.

"Dude, Hollywood is full of shit," Cheney said, finally grinning.

Cassell laughed, pulling out his smokes again. The cigarette's glow lit his face as he took a long drag, handing the pack to Cheney, who tucked a dip into his lip.

"Yeah, so...okay," Cassell said, exhaling smoke, "maybe it's not as quiet as I thought."

"Not a word, man. We don't talk about this, ever."

"Hell no. Say anything to anyone about what? I don't even know what you're talking about."

They exchanged glances, two idiots under the night sky, surrounded by the distant thrum of Ramadi and the soft rustle of sandbags.

Chapter 18

What are the odds?

Early March 2005.

Combat is so unpredictable. The taste of dust never leaves your mouth, clinging with a bitterness that becomes part of you. The acrid scent of cordite and burnt rubber lingers in the air, sharp and metallic, mingling with the sweat-soaked grime that coats every soldier. The city's cries—shouts, wails, the growl of engines, and the crackle of distant gunfire—blend into an unnerving background score, humming beneath everything like a cruel heartbeat.

Sometimes, enemy action can be anticipated, countered, and swiftly dealt with before any of our guys get hurt. But other times, fate is a blindfolded dealer with blood-stained hands, shuffling the deck without care. Today, that indifferent luck falls upon the engineers manning the checkpoint between Combat Outpost and Camp Corregidor.

The ECP, or entry control point, buzzes with the grim efficiency of war. The sun is a brutal, unrelenting presence, pressing down from a cloudless sky, bleaching the world in its merciless glare. Heat waves shimmer off the dirt and metal, distorting vision and mirroring the uncertainty of what lies ahead. Soldiers move in a syncopated dance of routine—eyes constantly scanning, fingers brushing rifle triggers, breaths held unconsciously. A truck idles nearby, its engine sputtering like an old man coughing up the last of his life, while a young private waves it forward, suspicion etched in every line of his posture.

Among them today is Command Sergeant Major Bergmann, "Birdog" to those of us who know him, a man whose presence is as reassuring as it is commanding. His gaze sweeps over the checkpoint, eyes narrowed against the harsh light, every step a declaration of experience and resolve. Unlike the tales whispered of ranking officers who claim the badge of combat from the safety of their armored offices, Birdog's boots collect the same dust, his uniform soaked with the same sweat and fear.

In the barracks, our platoon waits, the atmosphere thick with an uneasy sort of calm. The low thrum of a generator vibrates through the walls, accompanied by the muffled hum of conversations and the occasional laugh that cuts the tension. Sergeant Dubose and I recline in what we call our little home, eyes fixed on the grainy image of *Smallville* flickering on the television. For these few minutes, we let Clark Kent's scripted problems transport us away from the dirt and dread.

Then it happens. A dull, distant boom reverberates through the floor, rattling the flimsy shelves and dislodging a loose screw that skitters across the floor. One. Two. We wait for the third, the customary symphony of mortar fire. Silence instead.

The room holds its collective breath, the quiet now louder than any explosion. Dust trickles from the wooden beams above, an ominous snowfall that settles on our gear and the upturned faces of the men. My gut tightens, the sharp spike of adrenaline cutting through the temporary fog of comfort.

"Think they got anyone?" I ask, my voice low, half swallowed by the sudden stillness.

Dubose's eyes shift to the window, his jaw tensing. The question hangs in the air like a specter.

Outside, the ECP is a rush of movement. Birdog's voice slices through the din, an urgent bark that snaps the engineers into a rapid formation.

"Get accountability! Now!" The platoon sergeant darts among the troops, his eyes scanning faces, ticking names off in his mind as each soldier raises a hand or shouts, "Here!" Relief blooms for each one accounted for, but it dies quickly when a count comes up one short.

"Missing one," a corporal says, breathless, eyes darting toward the far end of the checkpoint. There, crumpled against the base of a Texas barrier, a figure lies still, limbs splayed in a position that speaks only of wrongness. Dust eddies around the motionless form, stirred by the uneasy shuffle of boots and the hiss of the wind.

Birdog's jaw sets, his fingers reaching for the binoculars hanging at another man's chest. "Give me them binos," he says, his voice softer now, a controlled fury simmering beneath the surface. He lifts them, the scene coming into sharp focus: the familiar desert camo patterned with dark, spreading stains, and the unmistakable sight of jagged mortar fins jutting grotesquely from the collarbone, embedded in the soldier's chest.

"You gotta be kidding me," he mutters, the words more a breath than a statement.

The platoon sergeant's brows knit into a deep furrow as he takes the binoculars. His face blanches, eyes wide as disbelief wrestles with grim reality.

"Holy shit, what are we supposed to do with that?"

Birdog's eyes harden, a storm gathering in their depths. "We should probably get EOD on the horn and see what they recommend."

The response, crackling through the radio, is both clinical and unthinkable: blow the device in place. The soldier's body would be reduced to a memory scattered on the wind. Birdog's expression twists, anger and grief mixing into something that seems to hollow out his voice.

"Okay, hell no. We aren't about to blow the mortar while it's still inside one of my men," he says, leaving no room for negotiation.

They move with the cautious precision of bomb technicians, crawling through the heat that scorches their palms and knees. The checkpoint feels quieter than it should, as if even the city holds its breath. Birdog's hands are steady, veins like cords running under sunburnt skin, as he loops the paracord around the fins of the unexploded mortar. The seconds stretch, elongated by the pounding of hearts and the prickling awareness of just how close they are to something that could turn them all into vapor.

"On three," Birdog whispers, his voice tight.

One, two. The paracord jerks, taut with resistance, then slips free with a suddenness that makes them both flinch. The mortar clatters to the concrete, a sound so ordinary that it takes a heartbeat to register its gravity. They stare at it, daring it to betray them, waiting for the detonation that doesn't come. It lies still, the nose pin intact—a mistake by whoever prepared it. The gods of war, for once, blinked.

Relief crashes in, sudden and almost painful in its intensity. The platoon sergeant exhales a shaky breath, securing the dud as other soldiers approach, eyes haunted, to lift the fallen.

Back in the barracks, our sergeant walks in, the story on his face. The muted sounds of *Smallville* still play in the background, absurdly normal amidst the harsh reality that sinks into us like shrapnel. A murmur cuts through the silence, a mixture of disbelief and sorrow.

"Man, that has to be the most unlucky guy in Iraq right now. What a damn shame," I whisper, the weight of it pressing down as the room holds its silence in shared, unsaid prayers.

Chapter 19
What a Bloody Mess
March 18th, 2005

2200 hours

Patterson bent down, gripping the 5-gallon jerry can filled with JP-8, preparing for the most gruesome task he'd ever faced. "What the hell just happened?" he muttered, unscrewing the cap. He didn't flinch as the fuel splashed over his hands. His bloodied uniform, discarded and soaking at the bottom of the burn barrel, gleamed under the faint moonlight. The air, thick with the stench of charred flesh, sweat, diesel, and smoke, would turn the stomach of most men, but Patterson barely noticed. Alone in the dim night, he flicked a match into the barrel and watched as flames surged to life, shadows dancing wildly against the barracks wall. He tore off another match and lit the cigarette he had craved since trudging back through the gate. Settling down, he cracked open a warm orange Fanta and took a sip, the fizz biting his tongue. "God, I hope this doesn't mess me up later," he said to no one.

Three hours earlier

The IED that hit my Humvee over two weeks ago had lodged itself deep in my mind, making every drive feel like a tightrope over hell. Inside the wire, I could manage, but on the roads, fear twisted into reckless speed and sharp, desperate turns. Sergeant Dubose kept scolding me and telling me to slow down, but I was convinced that if I didn't push it, another blast would come. Each day, it was getting easier, but I needed to get my head straight—this place was the Wild West.

A week ago, a VBIED exploded just outside our front gate, killing two engineers and an Iraqi commando. My platoon had manned that same checkpoint days earlier. It was the second time we'd missed a car bomb by less than 48 hours.

Today, we were on QRF again. Since moving to Camp Corregidor, we could stay in our squad rooms while on duty. The second floor of our building was crammed but comfortable enough, each squad wedged into small, air-conditioned rooms. The first floor housed a modest internet café, a luxury in this dust-choked city. I often sat on the stairwell leading up to the roof, guitar in hand, finding solace in the familiar strum of chords.

This afternoon, while playing, the battalion chaplain's assistant passed by and stopped to listen. He played too, and soon we were taking turns, talking about God, combat, and music. He had just started strumming when the world ruptured. The building shuddered, and the deafening roar made my vision blur.

"Oh my God," I gasped.

The chaplain's assistant handed me back the guitar, eyes hollow. It was the second time on this deployment I heard someone say, "I've gotta go help with the bodies."

Minutes earlier

Ragged bursts of celebratory AK-47 fire cracked the air, fired by Iraqi commandos elated to go home on leave. Their replacements, riding in on a flatbed truck, were moments from arrival. Every U.S. battalion was paired with an Iraqi Army unit, advised by a MiTT team. Their compound, a short walk east from Camp Corregidor's front gate, sat along the northern edge of Route Michigan. Built by our troops, it made joint operations easier. The commandos manned the checkpoint with us, and today's gunfire caused a brief, tense confusion.

Staff Sergeant Cantu, a Charlie Company Squad Leader on duty at the checkpoint, narrowed his eyes at a vehicle approaching. It sagged under an unseen weight, moving awkwardly. When the driver stepped out—clean-shaven, neatly dressed, nerves strung tight—Cantu's instincts flared. This man was prepared to die. He yelled for his men to take cover behind the barriers.

Using the gunfire as a distraction, the driver slipped back behind the wheel and floored it, tearing through the concertina wire. The car veered toward the truck, coming to a halt. A heartbeat later, the VBIED detonated. The explosion split the night wide open, sending a cascade of shrapnel slicing through the unarmored truck. The commandos in the back were torn apart.

Back on the rooftop

Soldiers scrambled to see what had happened, leaning over the edge. Flames billowed, twisting into a column of smoke. Twisted metal and burning bodies turned the night into a vision of hell. My gut tightened as I recognized the scene: Charlie Company. They'd been hit again. This was their third VBIED.

"Third Platoon, let's go! We're securing the area!" A squad leader's voice boomed from the stairwell.

I yanked on my gear, grabbed my rifle, and sprinted to my Humvee. The air was electric with dread, the smell of death already thickening. Patterson, gunning for the battalion commander's convoy, dismounted and ran for our truck, sweat and fuel smeared on his face.

"Get out there, Patterson!" Lieutenant Colonel Gubler yelled from the humvee.

We surged out of the gate and set up a perimeter. The scene was chaos incarnate. I stayed with the Humvee, scanning for secondary attacks as the others began triage. Shattered limbs and torsos were scattered like discarded rags. Blood splattered the barriers and soaked the sand. Sergeant Dubose grimaced as he stepped past what was left of a commando, his torso suspended in body armor, headless and limbless.

"Holy shit," he muttered to Patterson.

"Dubose, help with the driver!" Sergeant Major Bergmann's voice cut through the din.

Dubose moved, wrenching open the vehicle door. The driver's face was gone, obliterated. He and Bergmann heaved the corpse out, laying it face down on the ground.

"Flip him over," Bergmann said.

"He ain't got a face, Sergeant Major."

Bergmann blinked, stunned. "Leave him."

A soldier nearby attempted CPR on a commando whose legs had turned to mush. As Dubose lifted the limp body onto a stretcher, the skin peeled away in his hands.

Cleanup

By then, the rest of Third Platoon had assembled with black trash bags, not for trash but for pieces of men. No one trains for this part—collecting limbs and shattered bone like debris. Sikonia stared down, jaw clenched, at a torso he had to pick up by the handle of its body armor. Sergeant Miner bent over, retching after glimpsing the mess inside the truck bed.

Nearby, an Iraqi soldier was shouting at the LT, his voice cracking as tears streaked down his dust-smeared face. The desperation in his wide eyes was raw, a mix of grief and urgency. He gestured wildly toward the wreckage, the remnants of his comrades lying amidst twisted metal and pools of darkening blood. His words tumbled out in rapid, broken Arabic, hands trembling as he pointed at the scorched truck. The LT, his jaw clenched and eyes hollow, strained to follow the torrent of speech, the commando's pleas filling the air with a desperation that pierced the chaos.

Patterson stood close enough to catch fragments of the strained conversation, his heartbeat drumming in his ears. He heard the LT's voice, edged with exhaustion and resolve, break through the noise.

"They want their gear from the truck."

Patterson's jaw tightened, the acid churn of disbelief gnawing at him. His eyes flitted to the smoking carcass of the vehicle, a grotesque tableau of dismembered bodies, charred debris, and oozing fluids that clung to every surface.

"Are you serious, sir? It's a mess," he said, voice low, almost pleading.

The LT's gaze met his, cold and resigned. "Do it. That's an order."

A tense silence followed, punctuated only by the crackle of distant flames and the distant shouts of medics. Patterson felt the weight of the rifle in his hands before surrendering it, the familiar comfort slipping away. He exhaled, a brief moment of steel resolve, and stepped toward the truck. His boots sank into the gritty, blood-soaked sand, each step a battle against the bile rising in his throat.

He hoisted himself up, the slick surface of the wreckage greeting him with a sickening squelch. The interior was a nightmare made real. A glistening, grotesque film of pink and black matter covered everything, splattered across the benches, the floor, even the remnants of shattered windows. Patterson's heart thudded as he forced himself forward, each step sticking and pulling like the ground itself was trying to hold him back.

The duffle bags were there, barely recognizable beneath the gore that had once been men. Their outlines were misshapen, heavy with what they carried and soaked through with blood and viscera. He gritted his teeth and began tossing them out one by one, ignoring the warm wetness seeping into his uniform, clinging to his skin. The sharp, acrid tang of burnt flesh filled his nostrils, so potent he could almost taste it.

Every toss of a bag was a defiance against the horror that clawed at his mind. The work was mechanical, a reprieve from thinking about what his hands were touching, what stained his clothes and burned in his nostrils. When he finished, he stood still for a moment, eyes locked on a dark smear across his arm, realization seeping in like poison.

Hours later, as we stumbled back inside the wire, the weight of what we'd seen pressed on us like a physical burden. Eyes avoided each other, words caught in throats, silences spoke louder than any shout.

Patterson appeared at the doorway of our squad room, his figure outlined in the yellowed glow of a single overhead bulb. He looked like a ghost, uniform plastered to his skin with drying blood and the slimy residue of that truck. His face, usually animated with humor or intensity, was blank, a shell of the man he'd been hours earlier.

"Patterson, get out of here. You need to clean up," Dubose said, his voice rough, an attempt to anchor reality.

Patterson didn't react at first, as if the words hadn't reached him. Then, slow as a man waking from a long nightmare, he turned and made his way back outside. He peeled the uniform off, the fabric sticking like a second skin, before grabbing a nearby burn barrel.

The match struck, hissed, and flared. Patterson lit a cigarette and dropped the uniform into the flames, watching as they swallowed the black and pink stains, the day's horrors dissolving into smoke. Each drag of his cigarette came between gulps of warm Fanta, the carbonation doing nothing to cut through the bitter taste of what he'd witnessed. His eyes never left the fire, the orange glow casting long, flickering shadows across his weary face. He stood there in the quiet, the world around him dimmed to just the crackle of burning fabric and the distant echoes of war, bracing for the ghosts that would haunt his nights.

Chapter 20
The Phantom of Ramadi
Late April 2005

Days on Quick Reaction Force (QRF) detail are a strange blend of relief and tension. They offer us the illusion of downtime, the occasional break from relentless patrols and raids. If we're not called out, it's a rare chance to sprawl on ragged cots or makeshift seating, catching the latest bootleg movies or reruns of shows that bring echoes of a world far removed from this heat-scoured city. But today, as fate would have it, wasn't one of those days. Today, we were rolling out, and the rumors were electric.

The target? The most wanted man in Iraq, Abu Musab al-Zarqawi. The Jordanian jihadist whose name was whispered with a mix of rage and dread. Tied directly to Osama Bin Laden, Zarqawi had risen through the ranks of insurgency to command al-Qaeda in Iraq, pledging holy war on U.S. forces and preparing to stoke the fires of civil conflict among Iraq's fractured sects. And now, they said he was in Ramadi, maybe wounded, maybe desperate, and holed up in one of the city's crumbling hospitals.

"Why would a guy like Zarqawi risk coming into a hospital?" I wondered aloud, fingers drumming against the metal frame of the humvee.

The question gnawed at me. Was he really that bold, or had the terror of being hunted pushed him into reckless moves? The intel we received was thin, as always, but the stakes were high. If the rumors were true, we were one step from nabbing the shadow that had eluded us for so long.

Our orders were straightforward but heavy with consequence. Cordon off the perimeter while the SEALs went in. Well, I was told they were SEALs but to be honest, it quite possibly could have been another SOF unit. They were the scalpel; we were the sledgehammer, prepared to swing if needed. We sat idle on the outskirts of town, engines rumbling beneath us, waiting for the arrival of the special operations convoy.

Time crawled, each minute taut as a wire. I shifted in my seat, glancing at Sergeant Dubose who stood outside, arms crossed, eyes narrowed toward the horizon. The dusty wind swept across the cracked road, and for a moment, the landscape seemed frozen, as if the city itself held its breath. Then, with a low growl, the unmistakable silhouette of modified humvees appeared. SEALs. No unit patches, no names. Just men who seemed to carry the war itself on their backs, who moved with an assuredness that was almost intimidating.

"Sergeant Dubose, why does a SEAL team need an escort? I don't get it," I asked, trying to mask my nerves.

He turned, the corners of his mouth pulling into a faint smirk. "Stoke, don't overthink it. We're just here for the show." It was almost fatherly the way he said it, or like an older brother perhaps.

The SEALs didn't so much as glance our way as they passed, eyes hidden behind dark lenses, bodies shifting like coiled springs ready to snap. For a moment, I felt a rush of something akin to pride mixed with longing. I wasn't naive to what these men were capable of; their reputation preceded them. They were the scalpel, but we, the 19-year-old joes and hardened sergeants, were the ones who stayed in this infernal crucible day after day, bleeding into the sand.

After we linked up with the SEALs and followed them back to Corregidor, there was a palpable restlessness. We stood beside our trucks as they conferred amongst themselves. It was odd, almost surreal, to watch them, knowing that within the hour, they might come face-to-face with one of the most feared men in modern warfare. They moved in silence, their coordination seamless. There was no barking of orders, only nods, and clipped words I couldn't make out over the ambient noise.

"Any idea what team they belong to?" Moret asked, nudging me.

"Not a clue," I muttered.

We exchanged glances, sharing the unspoken awe that settled over us. The SEALs were untouchable, mythic figures who operated in the thin line between chaos and order. But as much as I respected them, there was an edge of frustration gnawing at me. We'd been in firefights every other day, sweat and blood mingling on the same cracked streets we were securing now. If it came to it, I knew we could storm that hospital too.

"Stoke, Moret, get to the trucks. We're heading out," Dubose snapped, pulling us back to reality.

I scrambled into the driver's seat, feeling the weight of the moment settle over me like lead. Moret clambered up into the turret, locking the feed tray of the .50 cal with a metallic slap. It was a sound that resonated deep, a promise of violence if it came to it. The SEALs moved out first, their convoy slipping into the arteries of the city like a predator gliding through reeds. We followed, the rumble of engines merging with the distant pulse of city life. Ramadi was awake and watching, always watching.

The roads felt narrower as we approached the sector near the hospital, the buildings pressing in like silent witnesses. Our platoon peeled off, taking up positions to lock down access points, while the rest of the QRF and other Army units formed the perimeter. Time became a slow, suffocating crawl. The radio crackled intermittently with updates from the SEALs as they cleared the floors of the hospital with mechanical precision.

I gripped the wheel, eyes darting between the alleys and rooftops, half expecting an ambush that never came. Moret's silhouette was sharp against the sky, eyes scanning, fingers poised over the .50 cal's trigger. Every shadow was a potential threat, every distant shout a possible signal. And yet, the only sound was the muffled thud of our own heartbeats.

Then, finally, the word came through: "Negative contact. Target not present."

A wave of both relief and disappointment washed over me. No gunfire, no insurgents bursting out of the doors, no shouts of resistance. We sat, engines idling, as the SEALs exited the hospital with their characteristic calm. The day ended not with the roar of battle but with the bitter taste of a near-miss. The newspaper reports days later would confirm what our instincts had hinted at: Zarqawi had been there, a ghost slipping through our fingers once again.

As we drove back to base, the glow of the city cast long, jagged shadows across the sand. I thought back to the moment I'd wished we could take the mission ourselves, the arrogance of youth whispering that we would have been fast enough, sharp enough. But now, with the city's heat pressing against my chest and the faces of my comrades lit by the flicker of passing headlights, I knew better. We were warriors, yes, but sometimes you needed precision. And today, the ghost had slipped away from even them.

We totally probably could have done it though. Just saying.

Zarqawi's dance with death would continue for another year before his end came, sudden and fiery, under the weight of a bomb. But that night, in the quiet aftermath of almost, we were just soldiers, dusted with sweat and doubt, waiting for the next time the world called our name.

Chapter 21

Leave

May 30th, 2005

"Man, you have no idea how excited I am to use a real, flushable toilet," I say, practically salivating at the thought.

A good old-fashioned, all-American, white porcelain throne in a climate-controlled, well-ventilated, pest-free, smoke-free, and bullet-free bathroom. It's going to be absolutely amazing.

Initially, I wasn't supposed to get mid-tour leave. Leave was prioritized for married soldiers or those with kids, which made sense, and Johnson and I were bummed when our Qatar trip fell through a few months back. But I'd rather have leave now than that pass we missed. I need this break badly. Civilians don't always realize each branch of the military has its own deployment lengths. The Air Force goes 4-6 months, Navy 6-9, Marine Corps 7, but for us in the Army, it's 12 to 15 months. On top of that, our unit deployed straight out of South Korea, where we were already doing hardship tours. Army guys going to Korea are usually there for a year without family, and some in my unit were away from home almost two years before Iraq. I'm single, so it's different for me, but I could still use a serious break from this place.

I have a new guitar waiting for me back home, an ESP LTD Eclipse, along with a Crate half-stack, wah-wah pedal, and a 16-track recorder. I'm stoked to play it. If I knew back then what I know now, I would've gotten a better guitar, a tube amp, and a software-based setup, but you live and learn. I'm also looking forward to seeing those

American girls I've been missing. We occasionally have female soldiers attached to us for missions—like that one time we had a female soldier carrying an M249 SAW. She handled it like a pro, definitely earned my respect, especially since I've struggled with it myself.

Once, on a mission, she had to pee while pulling security next to me by our Humvee. I opened the doors on the side facing a wall and told her it was the best cover I could manage. She squatted right there on the street, one of the most dangerous streets in the world, and I kept watch. Situations like that make modesty a luxury in the field.

Now that I'm actually on the plane, I finally feel safe letting myself get excited. It would be just like the Army to turn us around and cancel leave for some BS reason, but for now, I'm thinking about Village Inn banana cream pie, pizza, and Dr. Pepper—all the things I fantasized about on those long ruck marches in basic.

A few hours into the flight, I stretch out, finally kicking off my boots and savoring the small relief. Next to me, the female soldier does the same, and then, to my surprise, her foot "accidentally" brushes against mine. My heart jumps a little. *Was that on purpose?* I shift in my seat, cautiously testing the waters by letting my foot graze hers. Her lips curl into the faintest hint of a smile—yeah, that was definitely on purpose.

Before long, we're engaged in a silent, no-holds-barred game of footsie, our boots forgotten under the seats. It's exhilarating, the kind of thrill that breaks the monotony of combat and reminds you that you're human, still capable of feeling something other than stress or numb exhaustion. The brush of our feet, the subtle press and pull—it's the most innocent of interactions, but out here, it feels profound.

Is she breathtakingly beautiful? No. Is she even mildly attractive? Absolutely not. By deployment standards, she's a solid 4, maybe, but none of that matters. This isn't about looks or attraction; it's about warmth, human contact, and the rare reminder that there's more to life than just surviving the next mission. Our hands shift slightly under the thin airplane blankets, fingers flirting with closeness, touching each other's thighs dangerously close to the fun zone but never crossing into anything overt. It's a dance of contact and distance, need and restraint.

We don't talk, don't even exchange names, and yet in that brief moment, there's a silent acknowledgment that we're both just trying to remember what it's like to feel alive. Maybe she needs it as much as I do.

When I land in Wichita, my parents are there to greet me, and we drive back to Hutchinson. It feels surreal. Everything here is exactly as it was, but I feel like I've lived a lifetime in the past nine months. It's hard to explain to anyone what we've been through. I don't mind talking about it, but if you weren't there, you wouldn't really get it.

Leave goes just how I hoped. I spend time with family and friends, eating all the foods I dreamt about on the flight home. I've actually put on a few pounds since I deployed—believe it or not, and it's not muscle. I haven't done any PT outside of sprinting on missions when the time calls, nor do I plan to after this leave. We don't have time, and I'd rather spend it eating as many snacks as I can get my hands on.

Before I know it, my leave is over, and I'm back on a plane bound for Iraq. No one to play footsie with this time; I sit alone, praying I make it through the next few months so I can come home, finish up my enlistment, and move on.

Chapter 22

It's not that we don't want to follow the rules, we just don't want to wait for EOD.

Sometime in June

In the military, like in corporate America, there's a right way to do things: policies, procedures, rules that keep the chaos in check. Most of the time, these guidelines exist to keep people safe and ensure everyone stays on the same page. But combat has a way of making its own rules, bending even the most rigid procedures until they snap. That's why, sometimes, you just drop a couple of grenades on an IED and call it a day.

Yesterday

"My job description doesn't say EOD," Sergeant Hicks muttered to Sergeant Dubose, the worry in his voice clear and edged with a nervous chuckle.

He flexed his fingers restlessly on the stock of his rifle, eyes darting to the horizon where the city's jagged silhouette met the deepening sky. Dubose's jaw tightened, the muscles working under his tanned skin as he shot Hicks a glance, half reassurance, half shared frustration. The desert around us hummed with an unnatural stillness, the kind that sank into your bones and whispered that something was about to go wrong.

"None of us like it, but we don't have much of a choice, do we?" His voice was firm, but there was a weight behind it—a hint of the exhaustion that came from too many missions where routine could twist into disaster without warning.

The assignment was simple enough on paper: escort the EOD team while they neutralized a series of IEDs scattered throughout our area of operations. But simplicity on paper rarely translated to reality. Out here, IEDs weren't just bombs; they were specters haunting every road and alley, reminders that death could be a flash and a roar away.

Each of us knew what it meant to roll out, engines growling beneath us as we passed bullet-riddled buildings and the watchful, shuttered windows of homes. Escorting the EOD wasn't just about protection; it was a gamble. They had their bomb suits, robots, and finely honed expertise, but we had the job of sitting vulnerable while they poked at sleeping monsters.

Dubose shifted his weight, scanning the men around him—Hicks with his nervous energy, Patterson with his usual smirk that masked seriousness, Moret chewing on a piece of gum with the kind of focus that came when trying to block out nerves. I caught Dubose's eye for a second, a flicker of silent understanding passing between us. We were all thinking it: the EOD team might be handling the explosives, but it was our convoy parked right in the kill zone, a metal buffet for shrapnel if something went sideways.

The air was thick with tension, mingled with the scent of fuel and dust. The distant thump of mortar fire made the ground tremble slightly, a reminder that in this city, even silence wasn't to be trusted. The road stretched ahead like a promise none of us wanted to keep, lined with the remnants of yesterday's battles—craters, scorched debris, and the ghosts of ambushes past.

Dubose glanced back at Hicks, his expression softening for just a moment. "Stay sharp," he said, his voice a touch lower, almost lost in the rumble of the humvees. "We'll make it through this."

He didn't say *alive*, but the unspoken word hung between us like a talisman, fragile and potent.

Outside, I watched an EOD tech load their robot—a small, tracked contraption that looked like it had sprouted from a child's drawing come to life, complete with a multi-jointed arm and an array of cameras. I'd never bothered learning its name, so in my head, it was simply *Mr. Robot*.

We mounted up and rolled out through the front gate, following the route that had become as familiar as the back of my hand. Left on Route Michigan, past the roundabout, another left to Easy Street. The city lay silent in the sun's glare, shadows stretching across bullet-scarred walls. Soon, we reached our first stop.

EOD set *Mr. Robot* on the ground, its tiny treads skittering over gravel as it made its cautious journey toward the suspected IED. The minutes turned into nearly an hour. Sweat trickled down my back, and I shifted in the driver's seat, glancing over at Sergeant Dubose, who wore a scowl that said he'd rather be anywhere else.

"They're about to blow it," someone called over the radio.

I perked up, grabbing my 3.4-megapixel digital camera. But after another ten minutes ticked by, I realized EOD's "about to" was a flexible concept. My finger hovered over the record button as the countdown finally came.

"Fire in the hole!" echoed through the static, followed by a resounding *BOOM* that shook the air and sent a cloud of dust into the sky.

My grin stretched wide, adrenaline sparking. But no secondary explosion followed. They'd have to send *Mr. Robot* back out to check. And so it went, three more times until we finished for the day and rolled back to Corregidor, the street as quiet as we'd found it.

After Sunset

Hours later, darkness had settled over the city like a heavy blanket, cloaking it in a tense, uneasy quiet. The only illumination came from the faint, ghostly glow of our newly installed IR lights, casting eerie shadows that seemed to pulse with the weight of unseen eyes. The humvee engines hummed softly, their low purr vibrating through the seats as we sat at a neighborhood intersection, pulling security. The air was thick with the scent of oil, sand, and the metallic tang of distant gunfire, a backdrop to the restless shifting of boots and the muted clink of gear.

Patterson's voice cut through the silence, sharp and alert from his perch behind the .50 cal.

"Hey, Sergeant Dubose!" The tension in his tone was unmistakable. "I see something across the road. Looks like a wire."

Dubose moved with the deliberate calm of a man who'd seen too many things that shouldn't be there. He approached the road, eyes narrowed as he scanned the dusty pavement, every step carrying the weight of practiced caution. Kneeling down, he traced the wire with gloved fingers, feeling its thin, cold length disappear into a tangle of trash barely visible in the weak light. It ran straight under the lieutenant's truck like a snake ready to strike.

The radio crackled to life in his hand. "3-6, 3-1," Dubose called, voice low but steady, each syllable cutting through the silence.

"Go ahead, 3-1," came Lieutenant Chappell's reply, as calm as if they were discussing the weather. That calmness, I thought, was either reassuring or a special kind of madness.

"Sir, we've got a wire here that runs under your vehicle. It looks like it might be attached to an IED."

The seconds stretched, every eye locked on Chappell's humvee. The radio hissed faintly before his voice returned, measured and without a hint of the panic that wanted to claw up all our throats.

"Copy that. We'll move."

Dubose's knife glinted under the dim light as he carefully cut the wire, the soft *snip* sounding louder than it should have in the stillness. The tension shifted but didn't dissipate; it merely slithered along the ground, pooling around the mound of debris he followed the wire to. The pile was innocuous enough at first glance, just another heap of discarded paper and twisted metal. But out here, nothing could be trusted.

A quick exchange of words passed between Chappell and Sergeant Cromer, their voices a low murmur that carried hints of urgency. Cromer's face was unreadable as he finally leaned into the radio, his tone clipped.

"3-1, light it up with the .50."

Dubose didn't need to be told twice. He turned to Patterson, whose eyebrows had shot up to his hairline.

"Patterson, you heard him. Let's see what that thing's made of."

Patterson hesitated, the massive gun a silent beast in his hands.

"You serious?" he asked, voice tinged with incredulity and a hint of something like excitement.

"Yes, princess. Hit it," Dubose said, his dry humor cutting through the dread, if only for a moment.

The .50 cal barked into the night, each round exploding from the muzzle with a roar that rattled my teeth and thudded deep in my chest. The bullets tore into the trash pile, shredding it in a burst of ripped paper and shattered metal. I hunched lower in the humvee, every muscle tensed, expecting the world to erupt in a plume of fire and shrapnel.

But the night held its breath, and when the echo of gunfire died away, nothing stirred except the soft whisper of settling debris. Patterson exhaled audibly, releasing tension he hadn't realized he was holding, and leaned back slightly.

"Nothing, man," he said, shaking his head. "I don't think that was it."

Dubose's eyes didn't leave the pile, and the rest of us exchanged uneasy glances. The city, indifferent to our fear, pressed in on all sides, silent and watchful.

Dubose conferred with Cromer, their voices low and intense, a blend of urgency and frustration spilling from their quick gestures. The night hummed with tension, the silence pierced only by the distant crackle of static and the occasional thump of boots shifting on gravel. Then, like a dark storm rolling in, the first sergeant stepped forward. His eyes, gleaming beneath the rim of his helmet, reflected a mixture of determination and something else—something reckless.

"Throw a grenade on it," he said, each word biting the air like cold steel.

A collective stillness descended, the kind that locked your breath in your chest and made time feel elastic.

Chappell's brow furrowed in disbelief. "First sergeant, you can't just—"

The first sergeant's lips tightened into a thin line. "I'm not," he interrupted, his voice cutting through the night.

"Dubose is."

Dubose's head snapped up, eyes widening in disbelief. For a moment, the only sound was the faint rustle of wind tugging at their uniforms. The rest of them exchanged quick, sidelong glances, the unspoken "is this really happening?" etched into every expression. Dubose's expression shifted, a quickfire mix of defiance, resignation, and something almost resembling a dark humor.

"EOD isn't coming anytime soon, right?" he asked, his tone betraying a hint of weary acceptance.

"Right," the first sergeant confirmed, no room for argument in his tone. The unspoken words hung in the air like a challenge: *If you want it done, do it yourself.*

Dubose exhaled slowly, the sound almost lost in the cacophony of tension. He set his jaw and began peeling off his gear, each piece hitting the ground with a muted thud. His vest clattered last, leaving him lighter, more exposed. I could feel my heartbeat thudding in my ears as he nodded to Chappell. The lieutenant's face was a mask of forced composure, but there was a glint in his eyes that spoke of silent prayers.

I watched them step forward, shadows swallowed by the starlit gloom. Each carried a grenade, their movements deliberate but taut with the urgency of survival. They stopped, exchanging a final glance—one that said everything words couldn't. Then, almost in unison, they flicked the pins and let the grenades drop like iron petals into the darkness.

"Get down!" someone hissed, the words snapping like a whip.

Dubose and Chappell lunged back, boots pounding against the road as the frag grenades bounced once, twice, before a deafening explosion ripped through the quiet. The shockwave tore the stillness apart, sending a shudder through the ground and a rain of debris into the air. My teeth clattered together from the impact, my body pressed tight against the humvee door as dust billowed in thick, choking waves.

The seconds stretched, silent but for the ringing in my ears. Eyes squinted against the settling grit, I scanned the scene. No secondary explosion. No plume of fire. The grenades had detonated, but the IED remained ominously silent.

Dubose, undeterred, stalked forward with the steady focus of a man done playing games. He traced the wire to the far side of the road, sweat carving clean lines down his dust-streaked face. There, nestled in an oil can, sat two hulking 105mm rounds wired with det cord, the makeshift bomb's cold lethality now laid bare.

"Jesus," someone whispered from behind me.

Dubose worked with the precision of a surgeon, careful fingers dismantling the nightmare one step at a time. When he pulled the det cord free, it came with the blasting cap still attached, deadly and gleaming under the ghostly shimmer of our IR lights. He turned, jogging back toward the humvee, eyes locking onto Moret.

"Hold this," he said, thrusting the cords into Moret's hands, his voice calm, almost casual. "And don't let the cords touch."

The door shut with a sharp, final click. Moret's face paled, eyes flicking between the cords as if they might turn into snakes.

"Wait, what the fuck?" he sputtered, voice tight with panic.

From my spot, I couldn't help but let a snicker escape.

"You heard the man," I said, my grin hidden in the dark. "Just... don't let 'em touch."

He shot me a wide-eyed stare, fingers white-knuckled around the cords. "This is so fucked up," he whispered, a nervous laugh slipping through his fear.
Yeah, it was. But this was Ramadi, and out here, sanity was just a luxury we couldn't afford.

Chapter 23

Exfil

July 15th, 2005

Tonight is my last night in Ramadi, and I couldn't be more ready to get the hell out of this place. Ramadi will chew young men up and spit them out without a second thought. With seven men in my platoon receiving Purple Hearts for their wounds and one paying the ultimate sacrifice, we still fared far better than several other platoons in the battalion. Right now, they have us all sprawled out in an open field waiting for trucks to come to get us and take us to TQ. We'll be spending a few days there and then head to Kuwait for several more before finally making it to Fort Carson in Colorado Springs. I pray to God it's a safe trip back to TQ because it would be so awful to make it this far only to hit an IED on the last ride out.

As I'm lying here, back propped up against my rucksack, looking up at the night's sky, I get the crap scared out of me by what I can only assume is an American fighter jet making a low pass over Corregidor. It's one of the loudest noises I've heard in my entire life, and I don't realize until after it passes what is going on. While it's happening, my brain believes it's an attack of some sort, and I curl myself up on the ground, tucking my head under my rucksack. It takes a good 10 to 15 seconds before I look up and see other people recovering as well. Someone comments that the flyovers are probably happening to keep the bad guys away while our battalion gets ready to catch a ride back to TQ.

I've got to be honest, once we make it back to TQ, it's kind of a blur. We spend a day there before flying to Kuwait, where we spend several more days awaiting flights back to the States. Kuwait is also a blur because I can't think of anything besides getting home and living it up at Fort Carson. I don't think I could have picked a better base to come home to. It's close to the mountains and relatively close to my family back in Kansas, so I'm pretty stoked. My mom and cousin should be meeting me once we get back for our little return home ceremony, so that should be cool.

We stop at the airport in Shannon, Ireland, for a layover, where we can get off the plane and stretch our legs. They even allow us to have a few beers if you're old enough. I don't drink, but it seems so ridiculous that I just spent the last 12 months dodging bullets and IEDs, yet I am still not old enough to have a beer with my fellow soldiers. What sounds even crazier is that I only signed up for a two-year contract, so my entire military career will end before I even turn 21.

The plane ride home is long and exhaustive, but nobody cares. We are so close to returning to "normal" life that a long plane ride won't lower our spirits. When we finally land back on U.S. soil, a burden I didn't even realize I was carrying lifts from my shoulders, and my world is suddenly a bit lighter. Plus, right as we exit the plane, no joke, a dude is grilling McDonald's cheeseburgers for us. God bless America... and cheeseburgers.

With a cheeseburger and soda in my hand—again, God bless America—I board a bus that's en route to Fort Carson. Once at Carson, we step off at some sort of event center gymnasium and file into an audio track playing some generic patriotic country song, which I don't mind,

178

and are greeted by our families in the stands. There's a very short ceremony, and to my surprise, we are quickly released to go spend the next few days with our families.

It's so nice to spend time with my mom and cousin for a few days before meeting back up at Fort Carson. When we do, there is a memorial service for our fallen brothers that we all attend. Something also happens that I am thankful I am not a part of. The leadership of our fallen soldiers meets with their families to answer questions and describe what happened to their sons. I would venture to guess that no mission-sensitive information is given out, but it at least gives families some sort of explanation.

As I sink into my seat on the bus back to Fort Carson, surrounded by the quiet camaraderie of men who share every bruise and scar of the last twelve months, I look out the window and catch glimpses of a country that seems almost unfamiliar. Rolling plains, empty roads, and scattered homes—each scene feels worlds apart from the dusty alleys and fractured skyline of Ramadi. The weight of a year lived on the knife's edge dissipates with every mile, replaced by something I haven't felt in what seems like a lifetime: the fragile, fluttering hope that maybe, just maybe, life could be different now.

When we return to the grind at Fort Carson, it's almost surreal how life snaps back to the routines of formation, PT, and duty rosters. The Army has a way of pushing forward, as if it, too, knows that to pause too long is to invite ghosts to linger. My promotion to specialist brings with it a small boost, a tongue-in-cheek acknowledgment that I've become an expert at "shamming"—the Army term for making oneself scarce when there's work to be done. I smile, knowing that I earned every bit of that sham shield, every late-night patrol, and blistered foot along the way.

The day I clear post, my belongings boxed and ready for the next unknown, I look around at the mountains framing the horizon. The silence seems to hum with the promise of new beginnings. The life I'm stepping into feels like stepping off a ledge—an exhilarating and terrifying leap into whatever comes next. The military chapter is closing, but the ink has hardly dried before another page turns, leading to new enlistments, new paths, and the chance encounters that will come with them. Each decision seems random in retrospect, but together, they form the story I never knew I'd write.

And as I pull out of Fort Carson, the wind in my face and the hum of the road beneath me, I take one last look at the base disappearing in my rearview mirror. The place where young men came home as shadows of who they were, where we mourned, laughed, and dared to dream about the lives we might still build.

Maybe I'll be back someday. Maybe as an officer even. Captain Stokely does have a nice ring to it, but for now, the simple word "home" is enough. And so, with a deep breath and a hint of a smile, I drive into the open arms of whatever comes next, certain only that I'm carrying more than gear and memories. I'm carrying stories—stories that will weave through bar stools and campfires, whispered across late-night drives and quiet dinners, reminders of a time that will always be a part of me, even if I never return.

The sky stretches out, impossibly wide and clear. For the first time in a long time, I let myself hope that peace isn't just a word whispered in passing but something waiting, just a little further down the road.

Afterword

What a wild ride, right? People used to ask me if I had any problems or issues after returning home from war. Aside from feeling constantly restless and occasionally reckless, I didn't think I had many problems. I would always respond with something like, "It's crazy how two people can go through the exact same experience, and one comes out fine while the other struggles to handle it." I believed I was the one who handled it well—until a few years ago.

For years, I would tell people that I simply locked those emotions in a box, buried them, or shoved them in a closet and shut the door. And for a long time, I meant it—I was fine. But a few years back, that lock finally broke. One day, while driving, I was suddenly overwhelmed with emotion and started crying out of nowhere. I nearly had to pull over to regain control. Confusion and intense guilt swept over me. Around the same time, I began making more mistakes at work, and panic attacks forced me to step away from the nurses' station to collect myself in the bathroom. Eventually, I reached out to the VA and spoke with a psychologist over several months, which helped me find some stability.

Survivor's guilt hit me hard. I struggled with the loss of our medic and dealing with three of my squad members getting shot. The countless IEDs made driving an unpredictable and sometimes reckless task for me. But the deepest struggle came from an incident where I, along with a buddy, had to shoot the driver of a car approaching us. We never actually stopped to check if the car was full of explosives. It's one thing to fire at someone who is actively shooting at you, but it's another when you don't know if the person had any ill intentions. That mission never used to bother me, but as I've grown older, it replays in my mind: *What if that guy never saw me? What if he was just out getting food for his child, and now that child is fatherless because of me?*

I understand, logically, that it was the right call at the time—there had already been VBIEDs (vehicle-borne IEDs) earlier that morning. Still, it's a hard burden to shake. I value life far more now than I did twenty years ago. If you have friends or family members who went to war in their youth and faced real combat, they are likely carrying burdens you don't know about. And if you're someone who experienced combat, don't hold onto those feelings alone. Talk to someone. My experience with the VA was positive, and it helped me navigate some very uncomfortable emotions quite well. Stay strong friends. First Rock!